Mamacadabra

Mamacadabra

Poof! you're a mom now!

CARRIE MONROE O'KEEFE

MAMACADABRA PRESS

ISBN 978-1-7336299-3-5 Paperback
ISBN 978-1-7336299-2-8 Ebook

MAMACADABRA PRESS
MAMACADABRA.COM

For the people who (poof!) turned me into a mom —
Matt, Signa, and Sophia.

CONTENTS

Introduction

When our girls were littler, and I was newer to the whole stepmomming thing, I spent a year trying to improve our lives one day at a time. I wrote about motherhood, marriage, navigating the role of stepmom, and living as part of a blended family. I was told so many times to put my stories into a book but I wanted the girls to get a little bit older before sharing our lives with a larger audience. Now that they are successful young women in their own right I feel ready to share ourselves with you. I hope you'll be able to relate - whether you too are dipping your toes into the world of stepparenting, or you're a parent at all, or you're figuring out how to make a marriage, and a job, and kids, work within the confines of 24 hours in a day. Because lord knows *that*, in and of itself, is a magic trick we're all trying to master.

WINTER

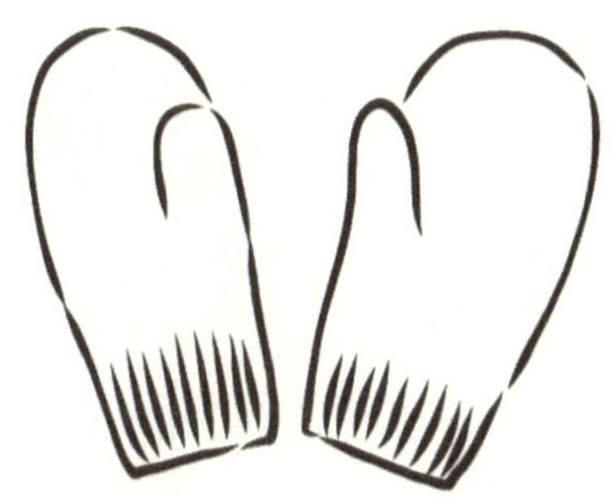

What If?

As I nursed a nasty holiday hangover, limping through my short work week, I began thinking about the upcoming year. How could I possibly have a better year than this last year? It's not like it was anything spectacular, but it followed a particularly horrendous couple of years, making it one of the most valuable and needed years I've had in my adult life.

So, I started thinking 'what if?' What if I took small, teensy steps, every day this year to make myself, my marriage, and my life, better? Little things, like doing 25 push-ups a day. Would 365 days of 25 push-ups give me Michelle Obama arms? I don't know for sure, but I can't imagine it would make my arms worse.

What if I woke up every morning and thought to myself 'I LOVE my job and I'm SO good at it!' Would I like my job more and more? Would I do better work? Raise more money? Again, I don't know, but I refuse to believe it could make me dislike my job or be less good at it.

To up the ante, I wondered, 'What if I wrote about it? What if I shared my idea with others?' Hmmm…it intrigued me.

I dubbed this idea The Year of What If and started talking about it with my friends. My girlfriends thought it sounded logical. Sensible. And dare I say…genius?

To be clear, I'm quick to come up with inspiring plans. Or any plan, actually, inspiring or not. I am also quick to let those plans fall by the wayside.

There have been a lot of plans through the years that were great, in retrospect, but didn't happen because I've just been trying to hold things together for my family. There hasn't been room to do anything extra. Energy for 'big, new plans' has been hard to come by.

Last year allowed the dust to settle, the guard to come down, and relaxation to set in. It took a full 365 days for that to happen. Now that it has, however, it's time for a plan. A good one. It's time for The Year of What If.

The idea went from maybe to YES on New Year's Eve. We were out with friends and after a few drinks my husband told some of the guys my idea about The Year of What If. These cynical bastards said that even if they woke up and proclaimed, "I love my job!" they'd still have to deal with the same BS they do every day. It wouldn't change anything.

I beg to differ. Right then and there, I vowed to try it. And then I decided to hold myself accountable by writing about this adventure and sharing it with you.

What if I wrote about The Year of What If? For the record, this totally freaks me out. But I'm doing it anyway.

Bring the Magic

Can we talk about this past Christmas? We've suffered through a few incredibly challenging years. And for some reason, we've just never had a phenomenal Christmas. Not the way I'm used to spending Christmas: happy, joyful, grateful, and feeling like everything is magical. This past year, though, we did it. It was happy, joyful, and magical. *Finally!*

Christmas is a big deal for me. I mean a BIG. SERIOUS. MAGICAL. DEAL. I love all of it. Shopping, wrapping, gifting, decorating, family visiting, Santa visiting, the bustle, the radio stations that play only Christmas music, my Christmas playlist, and it all begins with the trip to the Christmas Tree Farm the Saturday after Thanksgiving. Once that pine scent fills the living room, it's five fabulous weeks of anticipation, celebration, and joy.

Apparently, however, everyone does not feel the same way I do, which got me thinking about why it has always felt so magical for me. As I thought about it, I realized that a lot of other things I experienced as a kid were also pretty magical. It all leads to a single, common denominator: my mom.

I grew up with a single mom. She remarried when I was 12, but from the age of 4 until then, she and I were on our own. We were not rolling in the dough, if you know what I mean. But every Christmas felt like the best day of my life.

I'm telling you, things that I found at Fairs in the middle of summer would show up under that Christmas tree by way of Santa. 'How did he *do* that?!' I would wonder. I was so enamored with Santa that year-in and year-out I would ask him to please just send me an autographed picture of himself and Mrs. Claus.

My mom and I would Christmas shop, wrap gifts, listen to amazing old Christmas music by Bing Crosby, The Andrew Sisters, Frank Sinatra, and, of course, The Nutcracker Suite. We would make millions of Christmas cookies. We didn't have tons of family in town so often it was just us. It always felt like people were more cheerful, more kind, more excited through the entire season, not just the day itself. It felt like pure magic.

I found out the truth about Santa when I was in third or fourth grade. I was truly devastated, but my mom told me that the magic of Santa and Christmas were absolutely real. And by God, to this day, that is exactly how I've continued to think about it.

Mom's magic wasn't limited to Christmas. I felt it all year long. On New Year's Eve we would stay up until midnight to go outside and bang pots and pans together yelling "HAPPY NEW YEAR!!!" Every Valentine's Day I woke up to heart pencils, erasers, heart-shaped containers, lip gloss, and other cute red, pink, and white gifts on my nightstand.

On my birthday in March, we would have a party for my friends, but I remember her also taking me out for a special dinner. At least once she took me to a swanky old restaurant that seemed so sophisticated and fancy.

For St. Patrick's Day she bought green bread for the sandwich in my cold lunch (I think she bought the green bread, but sheesh, maybe she actually made it herself?). For Easter I would wake up and search for all the teensy piles of jellybeans that were hidden all over the house. Not to mention the bulging basket I'd find after collecting all the jellybeans.

On Memorial Day the Indy 500 would be on and she'd tell me stories about my grandpa when he used to work on pit road. I would sometimes visit relatives in Ohio for a week in the summers and one year I got home, and my mom had wallpapered my bedroom with fabulous floral wallpaper and found new matching bedding…I was shocked and so excited. The start of school meant extensive shopping trips for amazing outfits at JC Penny and Dayton's. Elementary school meant taking part in Brownies, and then Girl Scouts, and she helped me earn my badges. Halloween didn't mean finding a costume in a bag. It meant applying green face paint to be fully transformed into the Wicked Witch of the East.

Moreover, Mom worked in radio which, as a kid, seems like magic in and of itself. We were in parades in the radio truck. There were hot-air balloon rides in the station balloon. There were concerts, concerts, and more concerts. And I got to meet actual stars. Does the name Cyndi Lauper mean anything to you?!

The thing is, there was a lot of magic happening. And I'm telling you, it wasn't expensive magic. It was creative and thoughtful magic that made my growing-up years just plain wonderful.

I don't know about you, but there are days I get home from work and seriously, just getting through dinner and homework feels like running a marathon. Between activities, school, other kids' birthday parties, school carnivals, and homework, all we're doing is constantly moving on to the next thing. Where is the magic???

Wait, was *I* supposed to bring the magic? Son of a...

Children deserve to grow up in a world that feels magical and delightful. It turns out, the world doesn't feel so magical and delightful without someone who actually makes it so. It's dawning on me that this person might need to be me.

I'm sure I can think of little things to make my husband, our girls, my friends, and my family feel like a little magic is in the air.

What if I decide to make the world a little more magical for the people in my life? Even if I can make their worlds half as magical as my mom made mine...it will be pretty magical indeed!

Too Short

I think we can all agree that life is too short. Recently my little girls have been talking to me about college. Please remember, they're only seven and eight years old and we're talking about why people go to college, where people live during college (at home, of course), and where they themselves might go to college. Terrifying.

This morning at work, a colleague of mine resigned, and someone promptly escorted her from the building. On her way out, she told me she'd decided that "life is too short." Too short for what?! Working? Raising money for a living?

Later, this same day, I was checking in at the doctor's office and overheard an older gentleman talking to the receptionist about how he's leaving for Florida. The conversation went like this: Older Gentleman (OG): I'm leaving these cold winters and driving to Florida.

Receptionist (R): Oh, really? I'd fly if it was me!

OG: I want to fly, but I'm going with my wife, and she won't fly. Actually, I've never been on an airplane in my life.

R: Someday you will! *(said way too cheerfully)*

OG: I don't have much time!

Maybe this man in his 70s was being sarcastic, but it made me sad.

I'm thinking that I have a lot of power in how I live this life and it's up to me to make sure I don't waste my time. I don't want to wake up and realize the girls are actually leaving for college and be filled with thoughts of what I coulda-woulda-shoulda done differently.

I often think of where I want to be in one, five, or ten years in my relationships and work. All that thinking can get me caught up in where I want to be in the future, which makes me super impatient with where I am right now.

Logically, I understand I'm not getting to any of the places I want to be unless I lay the groundwork now. But sometimes I find myself going to work, staring at my computer, and thinking 'in five years when such-and-such happens I won't be sitting here.' Maybe this isn't a very effective way to move ahead?

My girlfriend Sara and I have spent countless hours talking about how we haven't been the best versions of ourselves. We get caught up in the minutia of life, operate at a level far below what we're capable of, and then we realize we've wasted all sorts of time this way. We're appalled we've been able to get away with it and we feel guilty about it.

Which leads to two important questions: why did we slip and how do we get back to being the people we know we can be?

If I'm a lesser version of myself, I can't imagine having the will, ambition, energy, chutzpah, desire, or wisdom I need to get to where I want to be in the future. Furthermore, what kind of example am I setting for the girls if I just shuffle through life with bursts of inspiration and effort once in a blue moon?

I want my girls to grow up dreaming big, sprinting after their dreams, and putting in the work to get there (even when it's tedious and heartbreaking and sometimes awful). I truly want them to be really, really, *really*, happy and satisfied.

Honestly, when I'm going through the motions, I might be "happy" with my life, but I'm not really, really, *really* happy. Definitely not satisfied. I'm restless, bummed out, and unfulfilled.

Life is short, but I will not sit down and write a bucket list or figure out how to retire in five years. I'll even spare us the question "what if we live every day like it's our last?"

Nope, I'm going to sit myself down and give myself a good talking to. Here goes:

> *Carrie, this book is a wicked awesome start and there's no doubt The Year of What If can help you improve your life. But unless you keep on keeping on, even when you're so, so tired, and actually put these ideas into action, it just won't matter. You're going to wake up in ten years, pack your oldest little girl up for Harvard (obviously), and wonder where all your dreams and aspirations went.*

Bottom line? Life might be too short, but I don't have to waste it. I have the power and opportunities to really live this life the way I should. I can become all the things I want to become. All I have to do is, well, just do it.

What if I stop wasting time and simply become the best version of myself NOW?

What if instead of thinking about where and who I want to be one, five, or ten years down the line, I live like I'm that person right this very second?

Charmed I'm Sure

Join me, if you will, for a trip down memory lane. When my husband and I met, I had a fabulous job as a fundraiser for an organization I loved. I worked, and worked, and worked some more. My accounts were sacred, and I did everything humanly possible to make their dealings with me and our organization easy, valuable, and lovely.

I worked all the time. I received (and took) calls from my clients on Friday nights, Sunday mornings, and before 7am on weekdays. I returned emails at 2am as quickly as if the message had come in at 2pm. I stopped at almost nothing to maintain my client relationships.

Not only did I love my job, but I was also fantastic at it. The companies I worked with raised ridiculous amounts of money for our organization and came back for more every year. The leaders within the companies were loyal to me and the organization. I got out of bed each morning with a spring in my step, drove to work with excitement and determination, and when I left each day, I knew I'd spend several more hours working from my home office. I felt successful.

When we first met, my husband and I shared this serious love of our careers. We both worked long hours, worked really hard, and loved that about each other. Truthfully, I was a workaholic, and he loved that about me. I was ambitious and driven, with a positive attitude about almost everything.

However, after the first lovely months of dating, the sh*t hit the fan. We were heading towards becoming a blended family, and right away we faced a lot of challenges. Especially with the heartache of sending children back and forth between two households, our easy and fun relationship became incredibly hard. It wasn't hard to be with each other…it was hard to deal with the bullsh*t that came along with co-parenting.

The following summer, I started to struggle. I fell into depression for the first time in my life and I didn't even know where to start to make it better. I was an instant mom, now living with my husband and his two little girls in their house, and found myself smack dab in the middle of a bunch of drama I wanted nothing to do with.

Because I couldn't accurately put my finger on just what was wrong (there was so much…where do you start?), I started to resent things at work. I know now I misplaced the blame, but all I knew at the time was that I started to really hate my job.

We experienced some devastating tragedies, got married, and my unhappiness at work grew stronger and stronger. Eventually, I started looking for another job. I found one, and probably knew deep down that it wasn't a great fit, but I pounced on the opportunity.

It didn't take long for me to realize it *really* wasn't a good fit. Before long, I was once again miserable at work. I wondered if I had effectively "forgotten" how to work. Or if I'd ever be happy at work again. When I was recruited by yet another organization I again pounced at the opportunity. I bet you can imagine how that turned out.

I emailed my husband 47 times an hour during the workday with random thoughts to avoid actually working. Each evening I'd come home feeling defeated, but I did my best to be in a good mood for the girls.

With me unhappy at work, my husband was at a loss. One of the things he found so attractive in me was my love for my job. My work ethic and drive. And to be honest, it's been gone for a long time. He wondered if I was just unhappy with him. Or with our life. Was it possible I just couldn't *be* happy?

We kind of figured out how to work around my misery with work, but it was never like it was when I loved my job and wanted to work hard. He did his best to cheer me up by acting crazy, or singing loudly, or messing around with our girls, and I would look at him with disdain and irritation. But we adapted, and I learned how to keep much of my unhappiness at work to myself or for my girlfriends' ears only, and he learned how to handle me.

Here's the thing. I started a new job the week of this past Christmas. Suddenly, the dread I used to feel upon waking up in the morning was gone. I spend my mornings with the girls, allowing them to sleep-in, listening to Justin Bieber, getting ready slowly, and stopping by McDonald's or Starbuck's on the way to the office. At night I either meet my family at the gym where I do yoga, or I meet them at home, or we meet for dinner. I go to bed at night without stress and without a stomachache because I have to go to a job I hate the next day.

In addition? I hardly even email him during the day anymore. I'm too busy. There are a million things I could and should be doing. I might work 12 hours a day and still not feel like I've accomplished everything I need to. And it feels f*cking amazing.

But here's the thing. The dynamic we've been working with for the past several years? It's gone. Poof! I don't need cheering in the morning. I don't need to be handled with kid gloves at night. And it kind of feels like we're starting over. Like we are in a whole new ballgame.

We might need to get to know each other all over again. The girl who loves working, who constantly thinks about what she'll do the next day to find more business, the girl who doesn't mind working at night, the one who actually (GASP!) likes her job? She's back. And I'm not sure my husband knows what to do with her.

Dear husband, It's nice to meet you. I'm Carrie and it turns out I can love my job and be an amazing wife and mother at the same time. Who knew?

> **What if as my marriage grows, and we change as people, we sometimes need to hit reset and get to know each other all over again?**

Stop Signs Don't Kiss Back

When I was little, it was just my mom and me. I had a lot of alone time. I had no siblings, and my mom worked a lot, so whether we were at home or at her office, I had to figure out how to entertain myself. No Nintendo Gameboys back then. To fend off boredom, my glorious imagination was born.

We lived one house away from the corner in the city. There was a stop sign on that corner. For all practical purposes, that stop sign was my boyfriend. I think it would be good to point out that not only are stop signs bad dancers, but they aren't very engaging boyfriends, and they do not kiss back. Oh, get your head out of the gutter. I didn't *make-out* with the sign for the love of Pete. I gave it/him pecks when I was *certain* nobody was looking. After all, I was only 8, or 9, or maybe 10 or 11. But no matter, ours was a secret affair.

There was a broom with which I was often forced to spend time (we had pine trees that covered our front walk and steps with pine needles, and it was my job to sweep them away) that became my microphone. I held concerts all spring, summer, and fall at which I did perfect renditions of songs like "Let's Hear it For the Boy" and "Lucky Star."

Our dining room table was the perfect location for me to make my talk show appearances. It was amazing how many people

wanted to interview me. A very young Oprah and Phil
Donahue, just to name a couple. It's tough to get to them
all when you're as famous as I was.

When my mom and I went shopping, I would bring along my
two sisters. We were triplets, they would show up anytime there
was a three-way mirror. Christine, Kate, and Carrie. We even
dressed the same. I assumed, when I saw other shoppers
looking at me, either with disgust or amusement, that they were
just jealous. Wouldn't you be?

Our concrete basement floor served as the hottest roller rink in
the city, and I would circle and circle and circle around the disco
ball (furnace) while thinking up elaborate story lines in my
head.

When my stepdad came into the picture and flooded an actual ice
rink in our big city backyard? Forget about it. We suddenly lived
in the North Pole, where I just happened to be a snow princess.

When my mom had me start ironing, I was a maid for a wealthy
family, and the very dashing and rich boyfriend of the family's
daughter found me very interesting and very attractive. He
wanted to ditch the rich girl and take me away from there.

I've always been a dreamer. I don't think one person who
knows me could tell you otherwise. Something happened in
college, though, that made the dreams seem less shiny and
sparkly. I can't say that I stopped imagining or dreaming, but I
can say that they were fewer and farther between.

Obviously, when things are dark in one's life, we focus on
surviving instead of thinking about what could be. I know that's

true for me. But as things have turned around in my life, I've had to work to get back into dreaming big. But I've also realized I don't use my imagination a lot. And that, my friends, makes me very sad.

Last week, the little girls and I were on our own one evening. We were going through the motions, "how was school, what did you learn today, what was your favorite part of today, and what on earth should we do about dinner?"

The girls had been asking to play restaurant for several days in a row and finally I relented. To be honest, on an evening with no homework or places to run, no excuses for why we couldn't came to mind. So, I gave in.

I sat them at a patio table on our front deck. I brought them water and a bowl of pretzels. Then I jotted up menus and brought them back down to them. They were really picky and took quite a long time to decide what to order. Damn customers. They finally decided on a fruit, a main course, and a dessert.

Okay, I'll be honest with you. I enjoyed myself. Are you kidding me?! I hadn't made believe like this since I was a kid. Unless you count simulated sales calls at company meetings, which isn't really what I would consider "making believe."

Back to the story. I went all out. I went back to their table as a normal waitress would and asked if everything was okay or if they needed anything else. I got a little crazy. I ran in and typed up little checks on my laptop. The girls had chosen different meals and so their totals were different. When I brought them their bills, they froze. My oldest little girl said, "do we really have to pay for this?" I said, "well, of course, but *we take credit cards.*"

I expected they'd get the point and run up and get their fake credit cards. They did not. My littlest little girl said, "I have money, I'll go get it. Will you help me count it?" Sweet little thing. After a few more tries to get them to understand, I was asking them to get their fake credit cards. I said, "GO GET YOUR FAKE CREDIT CARDS FOR PETE'S SAKE!" I then printed up receipts for them to sign for their credit card purchases.

They LOVED it. But so did I. It had been ages since I pretended like that. I mean, I guess we all pretend every day. We pretend we don't feel like crap and go to work, anyway. We pretend we're not mad even though we want to murder our spouses for not walking two feet to put their dishes in the dishwasher. We pretend we're financially secure even when we're a little scared about money.

But when do we use our imaginations and pretend for fun? I've talked about the need to dream big, but what about plain old use of our imaginations? Can we dream big enough if our imaginations are rusty from so little use?

Not to mention, if our children can fill their time with their iPads, their phones, and YouTube, and social media, how will their little imaginations develop? If we're not imaginative with what we talk about and do, is there any reason to think that they'll be?

I think it's time to bring the imagination back. For me, it will be like welcoming a dear old friend (and two sisters only visible in three-way mirrors). I can imagine myself in so many places (the Chanel store in Paris, for example) doing so many things (bringing the little girls to Paris) and maybe that will help me dream bigger and work harder at things that will actually get us there.

What if I imagine more?

What if I make believe with the little girls to really get their imaginations going? Sheesh! It seems like it will make life much more magical and lovely!

PS – For the record, my stop sign boyfriend never cheated on me while we were together. I never saw any other little girl spinning around him "Singin' in the Rain" style like I did. So, there's that.

Long Lost Me

Before I met my husband and became a stepmom to our two adorable girls, I lived in a fabulous condo. Alone. I decorated it with art and furniture that I loved, in colors I adored, and it had everything a single girl could ever want or need. It was a two bedroom, so I had a lovely home office, just for me. This is the place where I figured my sh*t out. I loved it so, so much.

I was working 50 hours a week in a job I loved, so I had the luxury of being able to afford my mortgage and buying the things I wanted. Shoes, clothes, eating out, seeing movies, golfing, cute golf skirts, cute golf shoes, shiny golf clubs, you get the picture. (This was also when I learned to play golf).

Because I lived alone, I could do whatever I damn well pleased. A weekend of binge-watching TV and eating takeout? No problem. Working until 11pm in my home office listening to loud music? Yes! Coming home, getting into jammies, and then being convinced to get gussied up again and meeting people at the bar at midnight? Sure thing!

I could spend full weekends not talking to a single other person if I wanted to. Talking to myself doesn't count, right? I spent days listening to jazz while reading books, listening to 80s metal and painting the closets, listening to 90s hip-hop and rap while painting my nails, and none of it bothered anyone.

I'm not reminiscing about all these fabulous aspects of living alone without remembering how hard it was when all my friends married and had children. I always knew I'd marry later. It was something I'd vowed to myself as a kid. But I confess, I got really bored when my friends had husbands and babies that prohibited them from going out with me as often on the weekends.

Still, the truth is I was truly HAPPY back then. I mean a satisfied-at peace-confident kind of HAPPY. There is nothing like that feeling in the world.

Fast forward to today. I felt like sh*t today. I didn't want to get out of bed this morning, and once I did I had this sinking, heartbreaking feeling that I sometimes get on the day that the little girls go back to their other house, and I didn't want to go to work, and when I got home from work, I didn't want to do anything but sit in bed and watch TV (like I used to when I lived alone) but the TV in our bedroom isn't working with our dish correctly, and it's a teensy TV and wouldn't do the trick anyway.

My husband had a work engagement that kept him late, followed by plans to get together with some friends later in the evening. We met for a quick dinner between his plans and then I came back home.

And then, my friends, something crazy happened.

The puppy and I walked into the house, our teensy unglamorous house, and I was *alone.* I had this weird sensation of déjà vu. I thought for a second about what I should do with myself, and it was like I was single again and living in my beloved condo. A house to myself, plenty to keep me occupied should I choose to be occupied, or there's always plenty on TV that could keep me busy. I could drink wine, or eat treats, or even head back out for a Diet Coke should I choose.

I sat down at my laptop to spend some time online and I felt like listening to jazz. Loudly. So, on it went. As I started online shopping (because obviously) something occurred to me.

Sweet. Jesus. I am *truly happy*. I mean a satisfied-at peace-confident kind of HAPPY. Holy sh*t!!! I haven't felt like this in a long time. I used to leave my condo in the morning feeling like I was all kinds of awesome. And I'd come home feeling like I was even more of a rock star than I had been when I'd left in the morning. Back then, I could be quiet and revel in it. Tonight, it's like I'm enjoying a reunion with myself.

For the past several years any quiet I've experienced has been interrupted by self-inflicted noise…either listing off things I need to do or have failed to accomplish or trying to make sense of the craziness that has surrounded us or struggling to figure things out. But tonight, I can just BE. QUIET.

Ahem…that is…aside from the whining of the puppy.

Note to self…all that talk of slowing down and living deliberately? Unless there is some quiet time involved, it just doesn't work. All the talk of dreaming big? Unless I'm able to be quiet to reflect and really *dream*, I'm not sure I can dream nearly big enough.

What if from time to time I make a point to JUST. BE. QUIET.

What if quiet time is one of the few ways to really remember who I am and what I'm about?

PS – John Coltrane is still allowed during this quiet time.

Who Invited This Broad

When I was single, I was the bomb. No, seriously, ask anybody.
I figured out what I was looking for in an ideal partner and
mirrored that. First, I started watching Sports Center. Yes, I
know, even the music irritates me, but watching 15 minutes of
SC a night gave me insight as to what guys would talk about
the next day. I would go on a first date and if the bar had TVs,
which they normally did, I could comment on something like
"yeah, how about the Giants?! Right?!" I knew just enough to
seem like a dream girl to any guy who liked sports.

I traveled a lot for work back then, and I like baseball, so I
started trying to see every outdoor ballpark I could when
traveling for work. I saw Fenway in Boston, Camden Yards in
Baltimore, Safeco Field in Seattle, Nationals Park in DC, Citizens
Bank Park in Philly, and Busch Stadium in St. Louis. I watched
games at home while I worked, so I had a baseline
understanding of the players and our record.

I even spent part of one summer with a magnet on my car for
the local team. Until I went on one date and the guy showed up
in an MLB hat, an MLB polo shirt, an MLB watch, and spoke
ONLY of baseball, and I decided I might be attracting the wrong
guys. Guys, take note: unless you are *playing* major league
baseball (and earning millions), you shouldn't be wearing *that
much* MLB gear. I'm just sayin'.

I learned to golf…okay that's debatable since I'm not even remotely close to being a viable golfer…but I try. Bought clubs, shoes, cute golf outfits (half the fun of the game if you ask me) and started golfing as much as I could.

And I worked my a*s off. I worked long hours, almost every night and weekend, and I was aggressive and successful in my job.

I was the woman that I believed the men I was attracted to would find attractive. And it worked. I had many guy friends, went on lots of dates, and ended up catching the eye of my husband because he had a soft spot for fabulous shoes (of which I had many). He loved that I golfed, knew and appreciated baseball, worked hard and loved it, and could hold my own across the board. I had a full life of my own.

What happens when you get married, run smack dab into rough times, and barely make it through in one piece? Things that are deemed unimportant disappear and suddenly there is no Sports Center (umm…no crying in my Diet Coke over this one), there is no knowledge of what's going on with our baseball team, work becomes exactly that, and it sometimes feels like there is no "me" anymore.

Part of it is kids. You have kids and your once free time is now packed to the max with kid-related activity. And it's fabulous.

But there are days when you wonder what happened to your former self. A couple years ago I was driving the girls to gymnastics. We were in a suburb much further out of the city than I had ever expected to live, blasting "Best of Both Worlds" by Miley Cyrus (or Hannah Montana…I can't remember), and both the little girls and I were singing at the top of our lungs. I looked around, surrounded by big box stores and cornfields, and thought to myself 'how the eff did I get *here*?!'

It took me awhile to reconcile who I was, with who I thought I was supposed to be as an instant mom, and finally the woman/wife/mom I actually *wanted* to be. And to be okay with all of it. Once I let go of what I thought I was *supposed* to be, or what I thought I *should* be, things got much easier. Because the truth is that I'm a million women all in one.

No, I did not say I had a million personalities. I haven't gone down that path of crazy just yet!

But I DO love baseball and would love to visit all the outdoor parks in my lifetime. I DO love working. I DO love golf. I DO love doing homework with the little girls (although there are days it feels like pulling teeth from an alligator). I DO love going to the outdoor pool with my husband and the little girls and pretending like it's our own…even if it means I don a swimsuit in front of a million other women and their families (and I haven't even had plastic surgery…gasp!).

I DO love going out with my girlfriends and having drinks. I DO love to volunteer at the little girls' school. And I DO love bumping around town in my truck or station wagon listening to Ice Cube or Frank Sinatra or Stevie Wonder or The Cure or Prince or (okay fine I'll say it…OR Demi Lovato or Selena Gomez or Justin Bieber) so loud it surely speeds up my impending loss of hearing.

I think it's important to nurture all the aspects of myself that I actually like. Because if I don't, I'm actually doing the opposite. And I'm not a fan of the uptight, crabby, and frazzled version of myself. She is *not* a fun broad you want to spend time with.

So, here's the thing…

What if I attempt to nurture all the "me's" that I (and my husband and my friends) adore?

What if I embrace those parts of me I don't indulge much anymore and really have some fun?

Eat Your Heart Out

You. You with the flowers, jewelry, and chocolates. I just want to let you know that you may have had a remarkable day, but my Valentine's Day was better.

This morning I woke up, sick, and needing to call-in to work for a second day in a row. My workload cannot withstand two whole days of doing nothing, so I got up, took the little girls out for a Valentine's Day breakfast, and came home to get some work done. After a couple hours, my productivity started to wane, and my mind drifted to Valentine's Day.

I realized that in 35 years I can't really remember what I've done on any of my Valentine's Days. How is that even possible?! I strained to remember something, anything, and this is all I could come up with…

Valentine's Day — Circa 1991

In eighth grade, I had my first real Valentine's Day with a boy. We'd been "dating" for about three days prior to Valentine's Day, so I was expecting something *big*. I wore a pleated, puffy, acid-washed jean skirt, a pink t-shirt with shoulder pads, my bangs were curled into a perfect ball atop my forehead and doused in enough hairspray to survive a hurricane, and I wore powder blue eye shadow and frosty pink lipstick. It was going to be *perfect*!

When I got to my first class and saw my "boyfriend," he gave me a bracelet that had purple and pink beads surrounding white beads that spelled out my name. It was magical…for about five minutes…until the bracelet broke, and the beads scattered across the floor of the classroom. We broke up three days later.

Valentine's Day — Present Day
Last night, we got our little girls back after being without them for the weekend. My oldest little girl's first words upon entering the house were "Momma, who is *YOUR* Valentine?" I was sick, so I wasn't on top of my game in terms of wit or humor, so I responded, "Daddy." I normally would have come up with something much more fun.

Oldest Little Girl: Who *ELSE*?

Me: You.

OLG: Who *ELSE*?

Me: Littlest Little Girl

OLG: Who *ELSE*?

Me: My mom, dad, and brother

OLG: Who *ELSE*?

Me: Ummm…

OLG: A *Valentine* is anyone you *APPRECIATE*.

Me: Well! Then the list is long.

OLG: I know, *RIGHT*?! (her favorite thing to say in response to just about anything right now)

It seemed so profound. As I drifted to sleep last night, I

thought I should make a list of the people I truly appreciate with all my heart.

Fast forward to my mind drifting and losing all productivity. When it became clear that staring at my work inbox wouldn't actually *produce* any emails with offers of millions of dollars for my organization, I began to wander around our house, and noted the following:

- Four loads of laundry need to be folded.

- Two loads of laundry need to be washed and dried.

- Dry cleaning needs to be dropped off.

- A single little girl's softball cleat sits on top of my book pile on my nightstand (Well, of course it does! Where else will it be safe from the teeth of the puppy? Never mind the fact we have no idea where the OTHER cleat is, rendering this one entirely worthless.)

- An end table in our living room balances on three legs because, apparently, at some point, one leg broke off. What?!

- A formerly lovely bathroom rug now sits in the puppy's toy basket and has no stitching around the edges.

- One of three framed pictures that hang in our kitchen is missing.

- There is a significant stash of fruit snacks, hair binders, and popcorn underneath our living room couch.

- There are hangers hanging on almost every doorknob.

- There are jackets, sweatshirts, and coats hanging over the side of *anything* that has a side.

Ugh. I cleaned, straighten, move furniture back into place, remove things sitting on the precarious three-legged end table, and the puppy took it upon himself to remove the cleat from my pile of books. I hit the wall quick; I am still sick after all, and quit.

I grabbed the little girls' Valentine's gift bags, grabbed my husband's gift and his card, and in the five minutes I had before running to pick the little girls up from the bus, I opened his card that I'd yet to sign.

That's when it hit me. While last year's Valentine's Day may have brought Tiffany boxes, and the year before brought new clothes, and I knew this year would bring…well…a new end table for the living room, it is still the best damn Valentine's Day ever. Because *this* year there is no concern for the health of my marriage, and the only job stress either of us are facing are simply the normal stresses of a job, and the little girls are healthy and so happy and such lovely people, and by God I'm doing something I love, and it is *amazing*!

I picked the little girls up, who were either on a sugar high, or just having a very good day, or both, and we ran to meet my husband for dinner ~~at a really fancy restaurant, at a semi-fancy restaurant, at a little hole-in-the-wall restaurant with character,~~ at Buffalo Wild Wings. We're nothing if not classy.

The little girls opened their gifts of pencils, lip smacker, and slippers with utter glee. My husband and I opened our cards, and, to our surprise, we found that we'd written each other nearly the same message. We then worked through homework over wings, cheesy fries, and Diet Coke (no, we do not let the little girls drink the junk). And it was…ridiculously lovely and peaceful…well, as peaceful as you can get with 97 big screen TVs and birthday announcements every four seconds.

After dinner, we got ice cream, rushed home, and got through the rest of homework, reading, showers, and bedtime. The little girls wanted lots of extra kisses tonight, which I'm chalking up to either Valentine's Day or their appreciation for their evening. And I told them each what I tell them every night, which was inspired by the book *The Help*:

> "you're a smart girl, you're a beautiful girl, you're a kind girl, and you're an important girl, and I love you very much."

I've been sick, and blue, and irritable all weekend. And while today included still being sick and seeing the current state of my house (truly horrible), it also included the kind of peace you only get when you're surrounded by love, and the realization that this…

This. Right. Here.

Is exactly where you're supposed to be. And it's *perfect*.

What if Valentine's Day is just a day to truly appreciate what you have (just the way it is) and those you have in your life (just the way they are)?

The Unicorn and the Elf

As a parent, a strict one at that, I do my best to try to control what my little girls are exposed to in their little worlds. For those of you who have your children with you all the time (no, not every second of every day, but every day at some point), you can do that to a certain extent. Imagine having them for half of that time, and as such, feeling like your ability to have even the tiniest control over their environment is limited. It's enough to get me breathing in a paper bag.

Our little girls go to a home daycare in the mornings before school and sometimes in the afternoons after school. They take the devil's transport, otherwise known as the school bus, to and from daycare to get to school. There are a couple other little girls at daycare with whom our little girls spend much of their time. Several months ago, I realized my thoughts on parenting and the thoughts of the other little girls' parents on parenting may not be the same.

When my oldest little girl came home singing "blame it on the al-al-al-al-al-alcohol", I realized there might be a problem. One little girl knows the songs I don't allow my little girls to listen to, the websites we don't allow them to frequent, and the TV shows that aren't on in our home when we have the little girls with us.

In my mind, although *never* out loud, this one little girl has become the bane of my existence. Arrgggh…WHY does she have to sing the REAL version of "California Girls" by Katy Perry when my little girls only know the KidzBop version?! Grrr…WHY does she have to sign my little girls up on this stupid website that I now have to prohibit them from using?! And seriously WHY is she so mean??? Ugh…a naughty girl in my little girls' midst.

Then three things happened.

1 - I was volunteering at the little girls' school recently, wrapping up a project in the library during school hours, and I sensed a presence. I looked up and the little girl of whom I speak was standing in front of me. She was wringing her hands, blushing, smiling from ear to ear, and she hesitantly said, "hi…hi…hi Carrie." It was precious. I mean, just sweet and precious. I leaned down and said hello, asked what she was up to, and after a bit, sent her on her way back to her classroom.

Hmm, this was not the behavior of a naughty little girl, this was the behavior of a little girl who wanted desperately to be acknowledged by a woman she knows from outside of school.

2 - Last week the little girls and I were driving, jamming out to the soundtrack from the TV show "Victorious" (you're so jealous of my music selection you can hardly stand it). Somehow, we got on the topic of the little girl mentioned above and my oldest little girl started talking about how her mom travels for work, in her words, "all the time." Oooofff.

And no offense to men. I live with a man who is a remarkable father, but there are days he will be channel surfing and will stop on the Sopranos when the girls are within earshot. You men, God love you, you're sometimes just not as aware of what kids notice, hear, observe, and pick-up. This little girl is spending all her time with her dad, who I know is a good guy, but who probably thinks nothing of letting her listen to or watch the things he's listening to and watching.

3 - Tonight, the little girls and I were practicing spelling words. One of them had a list that has words such as elf and elves, wife and wives, life and lives, and so on. When we got to the word elf, my oldest little girl told me that the little girl at daycare told them she was an elf. My little girls shook their heads like "here we go again with this little girl and her stories" and my heart just broke for her.

Primarily because when I was little, I had a friend named Jenny. I can't for the life of me remember her last name, otherwise I'd look her up immediately, but I remember her face (filled with freckles), her hair (Peppermint Patty red), and how she walked when she was a girl, and how she walked when she was a unicorn. I'm assuming you also know that people and unicorns do not walk in the same way?

Jenny insisted she was, in fact, a unicorn. Not all the time, only sometimes, and mostly, when I wasn't around. Jesus, that pissed me off. I remember thinking, probably much less articulately, 'Really?! You're a unicorn when I'm not here or just happen to be facing the other direction?! I'm so sure.'

She was hell-bent on it, though, and I'm pretty sure she'd convinced herself there was some truth to it. When she was a unicorn and graced me with her presence as such, she walked toes first with her head held high. I hate to admit it, but she was pretty graceful.

It irritated me on so many levels that even thinking about it now, while it mostly makes me sad, it also annoys me a little. Okay, first, you're damn right I was jealous! I was an only child, damn it. If anyone could use some mythical unicorn world, it was me, for Christ's sake.

Second, I mean COME. ON. Unicorns? I don't think so. But…BUT…third, she had the entire world figured out in her mind. The chain of royalty, where she fit into that org chart, what places looked like, and would tell extensive stories about it. It was so cool and yet so f*cking annoying.

Both of us had single moms. We met at latch-key and spent at least one full summer together, making up stories on the blacktop, and much of it revolved around this world she'd created. She had a dad around and, in retrospect, I think she was just completely desperate for his attention and adoration. I remember her telling me he would get angry when she would mention her unicorn world. She thought, or at least said she thought, it was because he couldn't see her horn or the other unicorns and was jealous. I assume now that it annoyed him that she never admitted it was make believe. She was committed to it like nothing I'd ever experienced before meeting her or since.

If as an adult I can look back and fully understand where my little friend Jenny was coming from and why she likely put so much effort into this imaginary world, I need to check myself and think about why this little girl who attends daycare with my little girls behaves the way she does.

I want to run to her house right this very second and squeeze her and cover her cute little face with kisses.

I said to the little girls, "she says she's an elf?" They nodded and my oldest little girl rolled her eyes. I said, "I used to have a friend who told me she was a unicorn but that I just couldn't see her unicorn friends when they surrounded me on the playground." The little girls looked at me with wide eyes and expressions made up both of disbelief and wonder. I told them she had one of the best imaginations I'd ever known anyone to have. And that I used to love to use my imagination.

I listed some things I used to make-believe (I may have left out the part about my stop sign boyfriend). Then they started telling me what they like to pretend. I told them I didn't believe you could be truly smart or wise without a big and active imagination.

In the real world, with adults, I usually have the wherewithal to understand that people are typically awful when they are going through some very rough times themselves. In most cases, I can step back and cut people slack because life isn't easy and all of us have our own sh*t to deal with.

When dealing with the little girls, however, I have such high standards for the people with whom they interact. I hadn't realized it, but apparently my crazy high standards extended to the seven- and eight-year-olds with whom they spend time as well. I have been bummed out that they've had to deal with this

little girl and have never given any thought to why she behaves
the way she does. Shame on me.

What if I remember that we all struggle in our own
ways...including the children with whom my little girls
spend time?

What if I do everything I can to add light to the lives
of children who may not have ideal home situations?

And what if I raise my little girls to be kind to those
who are sometimes challenging to understand?

Putting on My Own Air Mask First

We've had a tough week. We had to switch days for the little girls, which I loathe, but circumstances required that we do so. They've been much clingier, and needy, and snuggly in the past couple weeks. We had them last night, a day we wouldn't normally, and they were over-tired, a little weepy, in need of approval, and oh-so huggy. Yet at the same time, they were testing our limits. It's the kind of situation with which I could get consumed. Obsessed. And over-analyze until I'm blue in the face.

Let me paint a picture. My oldest little girl was finishing up homework while my littlest little girl was finishing breakfast. She hadn't touched her juice, so just after I took her empty bowl, she picked up the cup of juice and it spilled *all* over the floor, *all* over the table, *all* over the chairs, and *all* over the walls. I didn't see it, but the way the juice landed, I have to imagine she did something creative instead of it just slipping out of her hands like she claimed it did.

How it happened is neither here nor there. I can be a little uptight. So, I need you to understand how much effort it takes for me not to get mad in situations like this. But I didn't. I spent the next *fifteen whole minutes* on my knees cleaning it up and thinking of the note I needed to put in my littlest little girl's lunch so she'd know that I loved her despite the foul look I must have had on my face.

We got to daycare with homework done, vitamins ingested, breakfast eaten, teeth and hair brushed, rooms straightened, juice cleaned off every surface in the kitchen, even a cold lunch made for my littlest little girl (with the note!). My oldest little girl got out of the car and shut the back door, I grabbed the little girls' golf clubs that needed to be left and started walking towards the entrance, when I realized my littlest little girl was not getting out of the car. Hmmm.

I went back to the car, opened the back door, and said, "are you going to stay in the car?" And my littlest little girl said, "I want to stay with you." Oooofff. It's the worst feeling on earth when you're dropping your child somewhere and they don't want to go. "I want to stay with you," she repeated.

I got her into daycare, gave many kisses and hugs, and was on my heart-broken way. I first called my husband, then my girlfriend April, to lament that the girls were just needing more love than normal. Not lamenting that they need more love, I'm more than happy to give them as much love, attention, and adoration as they need. Lamenting about *why* they might need more love.

For the past couple of weeks, for whatever reason, the little girls need more of us. Require more attention, snuggling, and affirmation. We've had to step-up our game and be "on" more of the time. We haven't had the luxury of a less than stellar day of parenting because they're obviously in need of top-notch loving right now.

A couple of years ago, this would have totally consumed me. Speculation, anger, great sadness, it all would have put me right over the edge, which would have been counterproductive because it would have hindered my ability to be a great mom. Now, however, I recognize that for me to be even close to "on" all the time, I need to treat myself well.

I can't be the mom they need me to be unless I am the woman I need myself to be.

After venting with my husband and my girlfriend April, I came home and was swamped from the moment I sat down at my computer until the end of the day. Friday reports, phone calls, putting out a mild fire. It was go-go-go all day. Which, to be honest, was good for me. Otherwise, I would have been thinking about my littlest little girl all day.

Immediately following my whirlwind of a workday, I went to my dinner plans with girlfriends that I'd not seen in a while. We ate, drank wine, laughed out loud (perhaps too loud?), and had great conversation. I left the restaurant at 10pm. It was a *five-hour dinner* with girlfriends. And wine. It was so much fun, and I honestly could have stayed there for several more hours if not for the incessant yawning and overwhelming desire to lay my head down on the table to sleep.

So, here's the thing: If my little girls need more of me, if they need me to be on top of my game, if they need me to be their rock, then I have no choice but to be that way across the board.

Which means prioritizing time to be with my girlfriends and drink wine. Going to the gym so I feel good physically. It means

saying out loud all the things I want to be true and proceeding
to make them so. It means making sure my husband and I are in
a great place and are on the same page. Because without all
those things, I can't be the mom that my little girls deserve,
need, and are longing for.

It's like when you're flying and the flight attendants tell you to
put on your own air mask first. I must be in a good place myself
to provide a good place for the little girls.

What if in order to be the best mom I can be, I also need to be the best version of myself?

What if I need to cater to my own needs so that I can better serve the needs of my little girls?

This House is Not a Home (Currently)

It's a bright Saturday morning and I'm looking around my kitchen wondering when, exactly, I let it get THIS bad. The dishwasher has been run, but nobody has bothered to unload it, resulting in piles of dirty dishes in and around the sink. There are empty cereal boxes lined up, I assume, so *I* can cut out the Box Tops for Education labels…because I'm the only one who can what…use scissors? Break down the boxes for recycling? Throw away the empty bag inside the boxes that once held cereal?

Speaking of recycling, there's a bag of recycling on a stool waiting to be taken out on our "next trip" out of the house. It's been there for three days and we have, in fact, left the house several times in those three days.

The clincher, though, is the kitchen table. Our puppy has a best friend that lives next door. He comes over to our back deck door and barks for Sullivan to come out to play. They wrestle, run around, investigate, bark at each other, bark at passersby, lay down to rest, and then start over. When they're out and I'm working or writing, I bring my laptop up to the kitchen table so I can check on the dogs from time to time.

At this very moment, I'm sitting at my kitchen table and surrounding my laptop are:

- One little girl's black shoe.

- One little girl's gold shoe.

- One little girl's pink slipper.

- The Nancy Drew book we're currently reading.

- Large bag of colored pencils.

- Pair of my husband's dirty socks.

- Empty napkin holder on its side.

- The art project brought home by my littlest little girl.

- Pad of paper with my work notes scribbled on it.

- Three place mats (one was a casualty of yesterday's juice fiasco).

- One black marker.

- Work documents of my husband's.

- A partially completed drawing.

My kitchen table isn't even big! How, or perhaps a better question is WHY, is there so much sh*t sitting on it?!! And does anybody else find it a teensy bit disconcerting that there are two shoes, a slipper, and dirty socks on the table at which we EAT OUR MEALS? Anyone???

If I told you about the kitchen counter, you'd have a nervous breakdown, which I'm on the verge of, but I'm trying to hold it together. Here's the deal. We do not have the little girls this weekend, so we should be able to get everything organized, cleaned, and put away, but there's more…

My husband is in school. He was in school last night and again this morning. Also, have I mentioned he has a small business on the side that he's owned since he was 18 years old? After he bolts from school today, we'll be frantically preparing for his trade show tomorrow. Any 'free' time otherwise used for sanity-saving-house-organization will instead be spent on trade-show-preparation-in-hopes-of-finding-new-clients. Ugh.

Our dog is even looking at me with disgust. Yeah…YOU'RE one to talk, Sullivan…I believe that pile of firewood on our back deck is YOUR doing. It looks like the frigging Blair Witch Project out there.

I take issue with a disastrous house for many reasons.

A – When it's disastrous as it is now, I feel totally out of sorts and stressed.

B - It wouldn't be like this if *some people didn't* refuse to put dishes in the dishwasher, unload the dishwasher, hang-up their coats, put away their shoes, and so on, and so on, and so on.

C - We don't have the square footage to allow for unusable space…and as far as I'm concerned, this kitchen is NOT USABLE.

D - It's FREEZING outside which keeps us INSIDE this war zone of a house.

E - I believe our home is supposed to feel safe, and cozy, and comfortable, and lovely, you know, as opposed to chaotic, dirty, cluttered, and filled to the brim with crap people haven't put away.

Therefore, on a day I technically could have slept in, I've been up since 6:30 trying to get this house back in order. I'd rather be sleepy from a late night and an early morning than be CRAZY because the house is so awful. For me, sleepy is less dangerous than crazy.

Which brings me to the real question: is this my gig from now on? Husband in school, swamped at work, busy with small business, little girls here half the time, so while they're willing and eager to do chores, it only happens every other weekend, leaving me to take this on and be sure this house is in fact a home and I *AM* in fact sane? No, seriously…*REALLY?*

Chalk this up to a question for which I did NOT want the answer.

What if, in order to satisfy my need for order in my household, I actually have to step-up and make it orderly myself?

What if, because of the ambition and hard work of my husband (which I truly adore), I have to add the house to the list of things I need to take care of?

Wife (or The Amazing Kreskin) Wanted

Plain and simple? I need a wife.

Yesterday I left for work at 6:15am. I got home at 8pm. In between those ridiculous hours I went to work, saved the world, picked-up the little girls, plowed through homework, reading, spelling, dinner, gymnastics, and grocery shopping (while the little girls were in gymnastics).

Wait, let me clarify, I did all of this, and grocery shopped IN. HEELS. Okay, fine, I may not have actually saved the world, but it felt like it. I digress.

When the little girls were finally tucked into bed, I was exhausted, and my feet were begging to be taken out of commission. Which would have been fine if I didn't have to put away the groceries, make myself dinner, write, and prepare us all for another day (i.e., make cold lunches, make sure homework is in folders and in backpacks, put my briefcase back in the car, and so on, and so on).

It doesn't take a rocket scientist to understand I'm making this world go 'round. I smooth the road for my family, make things happen seemingly without effort, read minds, take matters into my own hands, and single-handedly manage *everything*. And yet, I'm starting to suspect they don't realize I'm doing it. I'm THAT. GOOD.

Listen to this common conversation in our household:

Husband: We're running low on rice.
Me: No.
Husband: Yes, we are, we're running low on rice.
Me: No.
Husband: Can you just grab some the next time you grocery shop? Oh…Cheerios too?
Me: Rice, top shelf on the left. Cheerios, bottom shelf on the left.
Husband: Yeah…well…I need pomade.

My husband and little girls needn't say anything more than "I'm getting low on," or "can we try," or "we're out of" and it magically shows up in their lives. I'm not talking about toys or gifts, but when it comes to necessities, I love being able to provide the things my family needs. I have a shopping app on my phone and I'm constantly updating it based on what I hear and see in my household.

Here's the thing. Sometimes a sister could use a little help. When I say out loud, "oh no, I'm almost out of foundation and mascara!" it doesn't magically appear within days. Even though my husband works two blocks from a mall where he could easily pickup both. I use skin products that are sold, conveniently, at a little shop across the street from my husband's office. And yet when I exclaim, "I'm out of face wash!" he doesn't run over the next day to grab me a fresh bottle.

Furthermore, when I talk about the fact that our house being in disorder makes me feel really stressed and overwhelmed, and he knows how much I suck when I'm stressed and overwhelmed, it doesn't inspire him to act. It's like…well it's like…it's like people have to be TOLD what to do. I would much prefer that everyone was adept at reading minds like I am.

I don't think I'm the only wife, mother or parent with a heightened sense of what's happening around me, knowledge of the habits-needs-desires of my loved ones, and an understanding of how it all fits together.

Most husbands? Children? They do not have said awareness. Apparently, you actually have to *ask* for what you want. With explicit details such as "can you please run the dishwasher *before* you *leave for work TODAY?*"

The trouble is, I also like to feel like I have everything under control. When I feel forced to ask for help, it feels both like I'm admitting I can't do it all (perish the thought!) and like I'm giving up a bit of control (eek!!!). Not necessarily in my nature.

But then I'm stuck. I get to a point where my foundation is a funny color, and it makes my face a little orange. I have to wash my face with a bar of soap or try to remove my waterproof mascara with just water (gasp!), and I find myself grocery shopping in heels at 7:30pm because I'm unwilling to spell out what I want and need from those around me to stay sane.

I want someone to pick things up for me if I'm running low (and it happens to be ACROSS THE STREET FROM THEIR OFFICE). *I* want someone to send *me* calendar notices of things I should have on my schedule. *I* want someone to listen to the words that are coming out of *my* mouth and simply act upon what they hear. I. WANT. A. WIFE. Or a mind reader.

And yet…truth be told…I will not get either. Sigh.

So, the thing is…I'm either going to a) do every single thing myself (as awful as it sounds…at least I know it'd all be done "right"), or b) ask for help and tell people what I want/need (blech).

But I need foundation. And mascara. And face wash. Sh*t.

What if I verbalize what I need my husband and little girls to do to help me get it all done?

What if instead of combing Craigslist for "wives for hire" I communicate with my husband and little girls?

SPRING

Mr. Big

I met my husband at Amber's wedding, the little sister of my girlfriend April. I was so tired of going to weddings alone. Those of you who are single, or who got married later, you know what I'm talking about. I was tired of buying gifts…alone. Figuring out what to wear…alone. Last minute card shopping…alone. Figuring out where to sit in the church…alone. Looking around at what everyone else is wearing (and realizing you're way over dressed…*again*)…alone.

Because I've known April since I was 12, her family feels like family. There were plenty of people with whom I could socialize. For the ceremony I sat with her younger cousin, who is ten years my junior, and spent the time trying to convince me I should be his sugar momma.

Finally at the reception, I did what any respectable girl who was alone would do…I started drinking. On my second (okay, maybe third) trip to the bar I ran into my husband. I'd met him before and had heard that he'd not only had a tough divorce, but he'd taken it incredibly hard. I approached him cautiously, re-introduced myself, and said in an empathetic tone *"how are you doing?"*

He looked at me like I was a crazy person and responded "ummm, fine? How are you?"

Hmmm apparently not willing to show how much he's suffering I thought to myself. We continued to talk for a bit and then the people I knew started to arrive and I left him at the bar.

At this wedding I was in my heyday. I worked hard, looked great, owned a great condo, and felt like I was on top of the world. When I sat down at my table, April's husband said, "that guy WANTS YOU." It may have been true, but he'd have to work a lot harder than he had thus far, so I shrugged it off.

As the evening progressed my husband tried to woo me. We danced (he is a remarkable dancer), he bought me drinks, he chatted with the people I knew (without an ounce of reservation), and I kept telling April that this was, absolutely, 100%, for certain, a BAD idea.

After the reception, a group of us decided to head to a bar and my husband tagged along. He and I spent the night talking. After the bar closed, we texted throughout the rest of the night. And all day on Sunday. We scheduled our first date for Monday, where he pulled out all the stops. And literally…we've been together ever since.

When I met my husband, I had an idea in my head about the kind of man I wanted to marry. Simply put, it was the character Mr. Big from Sex and the City. In fact, old co-workers had given me a framed picture of Mr. Big, and I had it amongst other pictures of family and friends on a shelf in my condo when I met my husband. I was looking for an overly successful, tall, dark, and handsome man.

My husband had, how do I put this kindly, baggage (I

am *NOT* including the little girls in what I consider baggage).
He wasn't sure he'd ever want more children. He wasn't rolling
in dough as a result of his divorce. He wasn't jetting around the
world doing real estate deals and could only see me on certain
days. He was not, to be perfectly honest, at all what I was
looking for. And likely not, to be even more honest, what my
parents were looking for.

But he was funny, and kind, and sweet, and took care of me, and
struck a perfect balance of putting up with my ridiculousness
but not letting me get away with anything I shouldn't (I have
the ability to steamroll people). And I adored him.

Frankly, we had a rocky start. After our engagement, a whole lot
of heartbreak transpired. And while our wedding was
everything we wanted it to be, it was also a very difficult day. So
was the entire first year of our marriage.

We had to deal with issues we never should have *had* to deal
with. Along with people we weren't particularly interested in
dealing with. My husband got really, *really* angry and I didn't
know what to do with angry. (I still don't know what to do with
angry.)

It was truly awful, but we made it through. And each year since
has offered a long list of reminders as to why we're good
together.

This year my husband has been more excited for my birthday
than I am, which is totally out of character for him. He's been
teasing me all week about my gift, which normally I would
love, but this year I've felt completely ambivalent.

First, he tried to get me to see the bag. Even though I turned around, wanting to save it for my birthday, he proudly announced "I know you saw it was a Burberry bag." My friend Sara started texting that she knew what I was getting. Then on Friday, he brought the bag into the restaurant where we were meeting his parents for dinner.

When I said, "I don't want to open it yet!!!" he brought it back out to his car, defeated. It became clear he was too excited to wait for my birthday, so I opened it a day early. What I pulled from that gift bag was a gorgeous merino wool wrap. Do you know what my husband said? "You're cold every single day in your office so now you can wear this to keep warm."

Sweet Jesus. This kind and thoughtful man. Who thinks of things like this?!

Amid our hardest struggles, sometimes my husband told me I could do better than him. But what I've realized after all this time is that I did in fact marry Mr. Big. My very own Mr. Big. Abso-f*cking-lutely.

What if what you thought you wanted isn't what you need?

What if you have exactly what you're supposed to have?

Her Mother's Daughter

My oldest little girl is the spitting image of her mother. To be clear, that's not me, she looks just like my husband's first wife.

I am the spitting image of *my* mom. We sound eerily similar on the phone, we feel the same way about most things, and sometimes when I'm speaking to the girls, I can hear her voice. I am her. So much so, that in business situations, I've run into people who used to work with her, and they've said "Chris???"

I know how cool it is to look exactly like my mom. I've been lucky enough to be compared to her my whole life.

As a mother to little girls who are not biologically mine, I sometimes wonder about my influence. I'm fully aware that I'm one of four parents and they'll soak-up the things I give and share, but at the end of the day, what will they really *get* from me? It's something that creeps into my head late at night occasionally, as I ponder whether I have any desire to have more children. Children that might look like my husband and *I* instead of my husband and *someone else*. Children I would be able to parent exactly as I see fit.

Our little girls may split their time between two homes, but they also have six sets of grandparents who clamor for bits of time, along with numerous aunts and uncles and a slew of family friends. It makes it hard for anyone other than the four parents to get real quality time in.

I'll never have conversations with these little girls in which I will remind them of things like "Gordy is my grandpa's cousin's son, you know, the one who owns the farm in Southern Minnesota." My Grandma in Phoenix is doing poorly right now, but the little girls have only met her twice, and thus explaining it to them might be confusing and feels futile. They might never be privy to family history that has been so ingrained in my own upbringing because there simply doesn't feel like enough time.

It makes me wonder sometimes what they'll truly *inherit* from me. When I start to labor over these things or find myself consumed with where I fit into this crazy puzzle, something always happens to set me straight.

My oldest little girl is in a phase in which she wears a tank top underneath any and every shirt. For the past couple of weeks, I'd been wondering why on earth she does this. I was getting dressed for work on Friday morning in an argyle sweater that is too low for the office. I grabbed a tank top, and as I was finishing my make-up, I realized that *I* wear tank tops under shirts. Often. To save myself from wearing something too revealing, to the gym underneath t-shirts, or just as another layer. *I do that!* My oldest little girl is copying *me*. I did a little dance in my bathroom because while it's trivial and isn't something that will last, it is, in fact, *something tangible* that I can see with my own eyes.

On Friday, after I picked the little girls up from the bus, my oldest little girl was using the word *infer* over and over again.

When I asked her about it, she said she'd learned it in the past couple days and wasn't it a *"good word?"* I talk about words, and language, and grammar a lot. It's something that was important to my parents as I grew up and now it's something we talk about in our household. The fact that she was so excited to share this great word she'd learned made me so, so proud.

And finally, over the weekend we've been celebrating my birthday and the little girls made books for me (I've made sure books in any shape or form are a huge part of our lives).

Each little girl referenced several times that they know how much I love them and take care of them. Oooofff. That children of seven and eight can verbalize that they feel *loved* and *taken care of* not only boggles my mind, but also makes me feel like the struggle, concern, and work I put in to being a great mom is paying off in spades.

Tonight, as I packed their lunches for tomorrow, I included notes that said my best birthday gift is being their mom.

What if what my little girls will inherit from me is a strong sense of feeling loved and taken care of?

What if that is more important than whether or not we share the same eye color or ancestry?

Tradition

Am I the only one who, upon seeing or hearing the word tradition, instantly starts singing the song from "Fiddler on the Roof?" I then break into a montage, in my head, of the other songs from that movie. And then I remember that awesome dance that Tevye does in the barn while singing "If I Were a Rich Man." Ahhh…high school movie days.

Since marrying my husband, I've been swept into his annual St. Patrick's Day traditions. We pull the girls from school, meet the large extended family for breakfast, and then we walk in the parade through downtown St. Paul with a large banner that says O'KEEFE. We do this in rain, wind, snow, or shine.

March in Minnesota: you never know what you're going to get.

I've been thinking about tradition ever since this year's parade. We didn't do anything in *my* family to carry-on any cultural traditions. But it occurred to me, we *did* have traditions. Traditions that I continue to carry-on today.

Whether it's the way we celebrate Christmas, or the magical things my mom did for me that I now do for the little girls, or simply carrying-on my family's strongly held beliefs about being active members of our community, there are traditions I've known since I was a little girl, that my little girls now know and consider their own.

Running is one of them now. My girlfriend Holly and I put together a schedule of runs that we do from April to November. The races range from 5ks to a half marathon. I know, right? We don't mess around.

Holly and I talk about wanting our little girls there to see us finish. We want them to see us participating in a community event and achieving something physical. We want them to understand that exercise is important and a big part of our lives, and we want them to see that we're strong.

No, not strong like winning the race (I'm loudly snort-laughing at that idea), but strong meaning we can overcome injuries, keep running even when it's hard, and we can train for something and follow through. Seeing their moms run community races can be a new tradition. One they can do themselves when they're old enough. Maybe even something they can share with their kids in the future.

I heard an interview on NPR with the author of *The Reading Promise*. She and her father made a promise to read every night until they reached a certain number of days. They started when she was nine and went until she went to college. I bought the book, and I *loved* the premise. So, the little girls and I made a promise to each other to read together every single night that we are together. Our first goal was to get to 100 nights in a row. We're now aiming for 300 and we're at 165.

I've heard them explain to their friends when have to come in from playing a bit early, and they talk about it with pride. Right now we're heavy into Nancy Drew books, and we read one chapter each night and then off to bed they go. Even when they're spending the night at their grandparents (on one of our nights) I will call, and they'll put me on speaker to read. We've never once missed a night since we made the promise.

The point is, we've created traditions in our family, and will be creating more that the little girls can feel proud of and excited about. They will grow-up feeling like they're a part of their community, have parents who love and adore them, and will have read 64 Nancy Drew books. What could be better?!

What if traditions don't have to go back years or decades or centuries, what if we can create new traditions now that the little girls will grow up knowing as an inherent part of their lives and history?

PS – If *I* were a rich (wo)man I would totally do that Tevye dance every morning when I woke up.

Seemingly Obvious Answers

When I was little, I had a strong need for reassurance. For my mom, that meant constantly answering questions to which I absolutely already knew the answers. About a year ago the little girls, more specifically our oldest little girl, started asking questions to which she absolutely already knew the answers.

"Are we going home?" (as we pull into our neighborhood)

"Are we going to the gym?" (as we pull into the gym parking lot)

"Are we taking showers?" (as I'm starting the water for showers)

"Did you go to work today?" (as I pick them up in my work attire)

"Is daddy driving us to daycare today?" (as I'm kissing them goodbye while they're still in bed in their jammies)

"Are we bringing Sullivan with us?" (as I'm putting him in his kennel)

In the beginning, it was so, *so* irritating. Seriously? You're asking me if we're heading home and we're like a block from our house? My husband and I kept asking each other what the deal was with the constant barrage of questions they knew the answers to. And then I remembered that *I* did that too.

I wasn't an insecure kid. I wasn't worried that my mom would leave me. But I did have a very strong need to know what the plan was at all times. And to be assured of that plan. I'm not sure if it made me feel safe, or more comfortable, or more secure, but I needed *something* from my mom when I asked those questions. The same questions we're now being asked by our little girls.

A lot has happened in the lives of my little girls in the past several years. And while we do everything in our power to provide stability and consistency at our house, it doesn't change the fact that a lot *has* happened. It's the reason I'm so hell-bent on our schedule and following through with the things we say we're going to do.

Every night I tell the little girls that they are smart girls, they are beautiful girls, they are kind girls, they are important girls, and that I love them very much.

But our little girls, like most siblings, are different from each other. With my oldest little girl, I sometimes feel like I'm trying to convince her. While with my littlest little girl she beams back at me and often tells me right back how smart and pretty I am. Like it's an understanding between two girls who are both pretty special.

In the past several years I've thought a lot about how my husband and I will go through life taking turns being the positive one, the strong one, the one really fighting for us. I haven't given much thought to how the little girls will need more or less of us over the years and likely at different times. Right now, our oldest little girl needs snuggle time, reassurance, and reminders of how special she is and how much we love her. She also needs reminders of how we, as a family, are committed to treating *other* people. Our littlest little girl, on the other hand, doesn't need as much right now. She's okay. She's getting more and more sassy (not in a disrespectful way…in a spunky way) and we laugh and laugh with her.

Over the past couple months, as I've felt like they've needed more of us, the days they return to their other house have been harder. I want to fold them up, put them in my pocket, and bring them everywhere with me. I want them to hear me talk about them, so they understand how much I adore them and how important they are to me. I want them to experience every part of my life with me. And I want to keep them close to my heart, so they'll always feel safe and assured and loved.

But the reality is that we have to give them up, over and over, and it's heart wrenching. All we can do is make the time we have with them feel safe, and good, and filled with love for our little girls.

Last night we had our first thunderstorm of the season. It appeared it was going to be a big one. At dusk, it got windier and windier, and the sky turned a dark shade of blue green. Conveniently enough, the storm didn't hit until we were mid-chapter in Nancy Drew and ten minutes from bedtime. Nancy Drew can feel pretty scary when there's a downpour, crackling thunder, lightning, and flickering lights. We put the girls to bed, allowed them to listen to *The Nutcracker Suite* in their rooms to help with the sound of the storm, and hoped it would pass quickly.

Thankfully, it did, and I began finishing up some work. Half an hour later my littlest little girl called out…

"Mommy? Is the thunderstorm over?" (no thunder had cracked in twenty minutes and the lightning had ceased)

"Yep! All over!"

"I thought so."

Then my oldest little girl chimed in…

"*IS* it over?"

"It sure is. It was a quick one, wasn't it?"

"Yeah…I didn't hear anymore thunder so I *thought* it was over."

"You were right! Okay little girls, it's time to try to go to sleep, see you in the morning!"

As I kissed them goodbye this morning while they were still in bed and in jammies, my oldest little girl said…

"Is daddy taking us to daycare?"

"He is. I'll see you at the bus this afternoon."

What if the little girls are asking question, after question, after question (with obvious answers) to feel more safe and secure?

What if simply continuing to do what we do, and answering their questions when they ask, makes them feel reassured and loved?

What if it's as simple as that?

Let it Go

It's not our weekend with the little girls but it is our year to have them for Easter. So last night we were able to get the remaining Easter shopping done without having to be stealthy, we were able to hide baskets and put jellybeans all over the house to be discovered, and early this morning my husband set-off to pick them up.

I've got a thing about holidays. I want them to be magical and memorable and *just so*. I was irritated that they wouldn't wake up here. I was irritated I had no control over whether or not they'd be showered when they arrived for a very busy Easter Sunday. I was irritated that we would likely have to rush them through their basket search and their jellybean collection to get them in their Easter dresses and off to church.

They arrived with unbrushed teeth, untouched homework, untouched spelling words, and having gone to bed late last night. I sometimes panic a little, inside my head. I do a pretty good job of masking it, but freaking out happens from time to time. WHY hadn't they done their homework (assuming we'd have a busy Easter Sunday planned)??? WHY had they stayed up so late (again…assuming we'd have a busy Easter Sunday planned)??? And…seriously? WHY wouldn't they have brushed their teeth???

There wasn't time to fret. Church at ten, lunch with my husband's family across town at noon, dinner with my family back across town at four, and then home to do homework (grr), practice spelling words (grr), and get our little girls to bed early so they are fresh (and hopefully partially down from their sugar high) for school tomorrow.

I can be a little, how do I say, *high-strung*. There are no ifs, ands, or buts about it. It's also possible that I have some control issues. I've told you before that the co-parenting can sometimes have me breathing in a bag. It requires patience, faith, and for me, an enormous amount of letting go.

Back in the day, and I'll be honest that includes even a year ago, I would have wanted to send an email. About just. About. Everything. I want (okay, need) people to understand where I'm coming from. I want us all to be on the exact same page with our parenting of these remarkable little girls. I want us all to hold the same things dear. Whether it be bedtimes or what we allow them to watch and listen to, or the kinds of things we feed them or how we punish them if it becomes necessary.

In the beginning I thought long verbose emails explaining our point of view would do the trick. Turns out those emails? They do *not* to the trick. They do the opposite of the trick. Which, in turn, makes me insane in the membrane.

It's amazing how serious things having to do with your children can feel. Simple things like practicing spelling words and bedtimes can feel like the MOST. IMPORTANT. THINGS. IN. THE. WORLD. Because all the things that go into raising children mesh together. And seriously, if it's important at one household but not at the other, well sh*t, I can easily convince myself that it's probably the end of the world as we know it.

Letting go is not in my nature. No ma'am. It's taken a good amount of time, a good amount of therapy, and a good amount of patience (something I also don't have a lot of), for me to be able to let things go even a little. I have these conversations with myself in which I ask 'is this important? Seriously. No, *seriously*. Is this important or is it just *incredibly irritating?!*' Usually, I'll decide that while *I* think it *is* incredibly important it's probably, in real life, only incredibly irritating. And thus, I have to decide it's not worth the battle and move on.

I've also really tried to figure out what things look and feel like for the little girls. I want them to feel like we all get along and that they are so lucky to have four parents who love them more than life itself. That means I don't get to react in front of them when I hear things that piss me off, freak me out, or simply make me sad. I choose to be positive so they'll feel like they can continue to talk freely about anything and everything. And so, they feel that between their parents, all four of us, things are good.

I knew the little girls were so looking forward to Easter. We hustled them through baskets, jellybeans, teeth brushing, getting dressed, and soon enough we were headed out to start our busy day. I was stealthy by encouraging them to bring the books the Easter Bunny had brought them along in the car. Reading? CHECK.

I also *happened* to bring math flash cards and they wanted to show off their math skills to their grandparents. Practice math?

CHECK. On one of the car rides we ran through spelling words to "get an idea if there would be any tough ones this week." Spelling? CHECK. And we were able to get home early enough to get homework done, allow the girls to play for a bit, *and* get them in bed early. Homework and early bedtime? CHECK.

They were able to eat seven tons of candy, don the most fabulous Easter dresses, sit-in on adult church and hear the most wonderful music, spend time with our families, and I was able to quiet the nagging voice in my head by sneaking in the things I felt needed to get done today. And I'm able to go to bed not conjuring up a ridiculously long email that will fall on deaf ears and instead, fall asleep while enjoying thoughts of a good day with my little girls. It's almost a win-win. If I can just let it go.

What if letting go of my control issues and my irritation allows me to be a better mom?

What if just making sure that the environment we provide is consistent and joyful and peaceful is the very best thing that I can do for my little girls?

And what if, in the end, the things I want to change and the things that make me crazy just don't matter a bit? Ooofff, I'll be honest, that's hard for me to even type. But nobody said this "what-iffing" business would be easy!

Money Changes Everything

Divorce is rarely pretty. Without getting into it I can tell you that when my husband and I began dating he was very hesitant to get involved with another person's finances and very protective of his own. While he loved me, he didn't trust me financially. It had absolutely nothing to do with me and everything to do with what he'd just been through.

After we got married, we chose to keep our finances separate. Completely separate. He would pay some bills, I would pay others, and we'd manage those bills on our own. We look at money differently, we manage it differently, and thus we have differing opinions about finances.

Some of the most horrific fights we've had were, on the most basic level, about money. You can imagine how awful it was when, after enjoying a year with our marriage on the mend, we were thrown back into intense money discussions after getting our taxes back (I'm sorry, we owe what???). It wasn't pretty. We both had flashbacks of our earlier money fights, and they were terrifying. Neither of us want to go backwards.

After many discussions about what the next year should look like financially, we decided it made the most sense to…*wait for it*…get a joint account.

No, I didn't say *merge* accounts, we opted for a new, additional account that is joint. This is an incredible win for our relationship and is also nerve wracking. Why? Because I'm anal as can be when it comes to keeping track of purchases and deposits. I'm old school people. I still balance my checkbook on paper and use the bank-issued check registers.

Yes, I'm that irritating broad at Target who holds up the line by writing down my purchases while still at the counter. How the hell will I keep track if I'm not the only one using this account?!

On the plus side, we're working together on our household bills. We get to sit down and determine what gets paid with what pay period for the next several months. The organization aspect of this makes me so excited! So why is there a part of me that feels like I'm on some kind of probation?

I realized that whether this goes really well or horribly, I feel like it will be a reflection of *my* financial competence. He's been scared to do this so now it feels like a test. MY test. I'm not particularly fond of this. I'm not particularly fond of having to prove myself due to someone else's irresponsibility and manipulation. It's not fair.

But…as my mom would say, "life's not fair."

My husband and I have long talked about how important it is to US to teach our little girls about money. We want them to grow up with a strong understanding of what it means to have money, spend money, and to do it responsibly and carefully. And maybe that's what this joint account is really all about.

The little girls started doing chores a couple months ago. With their help, I put together a list of things they'll do each day they're with us and every other weekend. Things like putting their dishes in the dishwasher, folding socks, and putting clean folded clothes away. They've embraced the chores with eagerness and joy. They love being part of the mix when we're "getting things done."

After a week of doing their chores, today during breakfast I wrote them each a check, and they just about keeled over with delight. I told them next week we would go to the bank and open an account for each of them. I then showed them my check register and explained how they're used. Since we're always working on math, I explained that it's just addition and subtraction. I told them that THEY would be in charge of keeping track of the money that is in their account.

Their eyes got big, they wanted to hold the check registers in their own hands, and when I handed them their checks, they stared at them in awe.

I think I'm going to look at this new financial adventure with my husband as a new beginning for our family. It's not going to be a year of vacations, gifts, and luxury. It will, however, be a year of feeling fiscally conservative and responsible, and teaching our little girls to do the same. And that's a little bit exciting to me!

What if instead of being irritated that I have to work at gaining my husband's trust financially I look at it as a new beginning and a new fabulous aspect of our ever-growing (and hopefully always improving) relationship?

What if our adventure can coincide with our teaching our little girls what it means to be fiscally responsible?

Choosing This

I always expected that I'd find some lovely man to marry who had a fabulous life full of friends, activities, and work, and that we'd merge our lovely lives and eventually find a house together in a community that we chose, and we'd have children when the time was right, and we'd live happily ever after.

It didn't exactly happen that way. I did in fact meet a lovely man with whom I fell in love. The rest of the plan did not match those early fantasies of mine. Because there were children involved, I felt like there was very little room or time to mess around. For the sake of the little girls, I felt an intense urgency to decide whether this was serious or if I should move on.

When we decided it was, in fact, quite serious I moved into my husband's house. The house he formerly shared with his ex-wife. The house *they* picked together. The house for which *they* chose paint colors together. The home to which the little girls were brought after their births. Needless to say, there wasn't much room for me in this environment from the start.

I was instantly a part of *their* life. Both the life of my husband and the little girls, but also the former life of my husband and his former wife. My so-called 'new' life felt like the life, home, and dream of other people.

This is probably why in the first year of living together, we took on house projects with a vengeance. I needed to carve out something fresh and new that belonged to me. At the time, landscaping projects seemed fun, siding projects were necessary, and we decided to freshen up a few rooms that hadn't been painted in a while.

Besides trying to find my place in our home, I was also now an active participant in a co-parenting situation. This meant more compromise, more settling, and more of my life dictated by people with whom I hadn't actually chosen to be in relationships.

Eventually we moved to the same suburb where the girls went to school to cut down on all the driving we'd been doing, shuttling back and forth to their other house. Since we sold our house more quickly than we'd expected, we needed to find a new house fast.

For months, we looked at houses several days a week and I scoured real estate sites constantly, all while dreaming about and secretly looking at houses in the parts of the city I *actually* wanted to live. It was so frustrating to know how many great options there were in our price range over there, even though it wouldn't alleviate the travel time the girls were enduring each day.

Finally, I found the house and knew it was "the one" when I first drove past it. It was a few blocks one way from school, a few blocks the other from church, and it sits on an acre and a half of land ensuring we can build our dreamhouse. Someday.

Even after we moved in, I spent the first year so pissed that this was where we lived. I resented the gravel road that runs through the back portion of our neighborhood. I hated the sounds of farm equipment on my evening walks. I glared at the horses I passed on my way to work each day. I spent more mornings than I care to remember thinking 'what the f*ck am I doing HERE?!'

In the past week someone made a comment, offhandedly, that I didn't make many choices in our early years. I don't remember who said it, in what context, or even when the conversation happened…but it sure stuck with me.

Lately I've been thinking a lot about choice. In retrospect, it's easy to understand why I felt so unhappy and why my husband and I suffered so much in our early days of marriage. Looking back, I realize how very out of control I felt. I met a man, fell in love, and was nearly immediately plopped into his life.

All the choices I'd made before that to create a fabulous life for my own damn self fell by the wayside. My condo, my choice of community, my freedom, all disappeared when I chose to live in someone else's house, help raise someone else's children, date someone else's former husband, do someone else's dishes which were probably someone else's wedding gifts, and make decisions based on someone else's already established decisions.

At the time, I really didn't feel like I was making any of the choices that were shaping my life. And yet, I've realized something very important. Something that changes everything.

I chose to be with this man.
I chose to become another mom to these precious little girls.
I chose to enter their lives knowing it would be a challenge,

knowing it was not the road I (or my family and friends) thought I would travel, knowing damn well that it had the potential to get very ugly.

I chose to stay when it DID get ugly.

I chose to stay when it got even uglier than I could have imagined.

I chose to stop the madness the little girls were experiencing sitting in the car for long periods of time.

I chose this house on this piece of land in this neighborhood.

I chose to be THIS wife to THIS husband and mother to THESE little girls.

I did that. Regardless of the pain, sorrow, depression, and the feeling that I was living in someone else's world, I made all those choices. Every day, I continue to choose to be the mom and wife that I am.

I no longer feel like I'm in someone else's world. I feel like I'm living in *my* world. With *my* little girls. And now when I walk in the evenings, I love that I can see all the stars, hear the farmers hard at work, and walk part of my route on red, dusty, gravel. And when we pass the horses, I point them out to the little girls with wonder.

What if some of the choices in the past several years were in fact MY choices? What if some of those choices are the reasons we are in the good place we are today?

And what if I make a commitment to actively choose the kind of life I live each and every day?

A Real Mom After All

This morning my little girls surprised me with breakfast and gifts in bed. Breakfast was an Egg McMuffin and hash browns on a plate and a 32-ounce Diet Coke from McDonalds. It was perfect. Their gifts included two bottles of perfume, several packs of gum I'd previously purchased for them, and several individual pieces of gum from packs they'd already opened. Oh, and a rock and a quarter. They made me cards and sat smiling and wide-eyed as I read each one.

I came into my little girls lives just after they'd turned three and four. The first couple of years were a challenge for me. Not because they didn't love me, or behave, or treat me like one of their moms. They were challenging because I was so unsure of myself *as* a mom. Everything was tough.

When I first started bringing my little girls to daycare, I felt judged and hated by the teachers. I'd go to pick them up, and they'd throw a fit because they wanted to stay and play, and I didn't know how to discipline them in front of all these professional childcare providers who clearly thought I was inept already.

I was nervous interacting with the girls in front of my husband's family because I wasn't his ex-wife, and I wasn't their mom. I never knew if I was behaving the way I should. I always felt an enormous pressure to be a good enough mom, yet felt like I wasn't a mom at all.

The first time my littlest little girl told me she loved me, we were in Target looking for tights for their Christmas outfits. We were circling the socks-underwear-tights area in the children's section and the littlest little girl yelled at me from the cart to tell me she loved me. Out of the blue. I turned and saw her looking at me expectantly. I looked around at the other shoppers, expecting them to somehow know I wasn't the mom, and of course none of them were paying any attention to us. I looked back to my littlest little girl and said quietly "I love you too."

She was still a toddler and was still going through a stubborn stage. She tested me from the moment I entered the picture. When I asked her to do things, she had no desire or interest in doing, she would stomp her feet and cross her arms. While the first few months with her were tricky, she came around, and soon she was undeniably in love with me. A snuggler, and hugger, and little lover, we found a way to belong to each other.

My oldest little girl took a little more time. Having just turned four, going on 18, she was like a little mom herself. She helped her little sister get ready in the morning, helped her with her shoes, and was a little helper to me and her dad. At daycare she always helped our daycare provider with the babies. She wanted to be perfect in everything she did.

But she also wanted me to know that she remembered when her mom lived in our house. When she was upset with me, she would cry for her mom. Nothing compares to hearing your stepchildren sob for their *real* mom. I felt like a failure and an imposter, and worried she'd never accept me as one of her moms.

My oldest little girl is smart and has an old soul, so we did a lot of talking. Regardless of her early tactics, eventually she came around too. Surprisingly I now see me in her so often. She is a spitting image of her mom but there are days that I look at her, or listen to her playing in her room, and it is like looking at myself as a little girl. Dramatic, imaginative, creative, and so bright. We belong to each other now, too.

No one can fully prepare you for the journey of being a stepmom. In the early days, I doubted myself daily, suffered from depression, considered divorce, and constantly questioned the meaning and viability of our relationship. My relationship with my little girls that is.

I had to look at the kind of mom I wanted to be and the kind of mom I actually was. Because we only have our little girls half the time, I was consumed with worry about what their life was like when they weren't with us. However, this only led to me being too uptight, too rigid, and too crabby. When they came home, the worry subsided but then I turned into a crazy mom, constantly trying to have everything work perfectly. Which, obviously, isn't a thing.

It took a while, but eventually everything just kind of fell into place. I stopped worrying what people thought about how I parent. I stopped caring whether others viewed me as one of the little girls' moms. Most importantly, I stopped trying to compare myself to someone else. Finally, I decided I was one of their parents and I *do,* in fact, matter. I'm playing an important part in how these little girls will grow up, how they'll turn out and who they'll become. *I am one of their moms.*

Reading the girl's cards this morning I was struck by their adoration for me. I can see and feel that they feel truly loved and taken care of by me. There's nothing I want them to know more than that I love them. And there's nothing I want them to feel more than truly cared for. No gift or Mother's Day activities can be better than getting confirmation that they do in fact know and feel those things.

When I realize how beautiful and strong our connection is, it allows me to let out a deep breath, sit back, and relax. In this chaos that is my life, and in the chaos that is the life of my little girls, I must be doing *something* right. Phew!

What if I allow myself to bask in the great job that I'm doing as a mom (their words not mine)?

What if despite my not having given birth to them I am a real mom after all?

The Mrs.

When I was little, as far back as kindergarten, there were boys I considered good enough to marry. Not many, mind you, I was incredibly picky, but they existed. Like other girls, I spent time attaching these boys' last names with mine.

Michael & Carrie Grover: we got in trouble in kindergarten for talking too much and he was so dang cute! Kevin & Carrie Johnson: also, super cute. We were in 'gifted' classes together in third grade.

Through my senior year in high school, I was still attaching boyfriends' names to my own. Even though many people in my high school called me Monroe, I still had no plans to hold onto the name. My senior year boyfriend and I had big plans to get married. We even had our neighborhood picked out. And I planned to take his name. *For certain*. Hold please, while I swoon over my high school romance for a couple seconds.

I started my career when I was 19. I started in my field as an admin assistant and made important contacts I still have today. As my career took off, and I kept getting better and better positions, I found myself in the enviable position of making a small name for myself. I got to know a lot of people and I worked hard to maintain a fabulous reputation. All as Carrie Monroe.

I still thought about the man I'd marry someday. I hoped I'd get some lovely last name that had character. You know, something like Carrie Del Toro, or Carrie Katzenberg, or Carrie Rossellini, or Carrie O'Donnell. All good viable options.

My friends got married, I remained single, and kept working, working, working. And then at 31, I *finally* met my husband. We dated for a year, got engaged, and then, we were driving home one day and started talking about whether or not I would take his name. Faced with the reality of changing my name, suddenly it wasn't about his fabulous Irish name and how it would sound after Carrie. Now it was real, it was very personal, and very, *very* difficult.

When my parents divorced, I was quite young. My mom had the choice of keeping her married name or going back to her maiden name. She had established herself in her career, and she wanted me to have a parent with my same last name, so she kept Monroe. When she remarried, I was 12, and again, she kept Monroe.

I grew up with a woman who always preferred Ms. to Mrs. A woman who was incredibly independent and strong. Someone who had blazed a trail in her career and always had her very own last name, the one that I shared.

When I told my husband I wasn't sure I could take his name he didn't understand. We went in circles. I asked if he'd be willing to take my last name (I didn't want him to…I was trying to prove a point) and he scoffed. He seriously looked at me like I was straight-up CRAZY. I tried to explain that it was the same for me. At 31, my name had become a part of who I was. Both professionally and personally, it was part of me. Just as I would never expect my husband to simply throw his last name to the wind, I didn't feel like he should expect that of me.

This all sparked a whole debate with myself about how I would do this. I knew I wanted the little girls to have a woman in their life with their last name, but I didn't want to mess around with hyphens. I wasn't willing to drop my middle name to be replaced by my maiden name. Why should I have to give up part of my name, my history, or my identity to get married? My husband came around and began to understand. After all was said and done, I became Carrie Christine Monroe O'Keefe.

Last week I chaperoned a field trip for my littlest little girl. When I arrived, I was handed a packet, and inside was a nametag sticker that read "Mrs. O'Keefe."

At first I thought 'wait…what? Seriously?' And then I thought 'holy hell…I have to send my husband a picture of this!' Which I did, obviously. Then I stuck it on my chest and started chasing six second graders around the Science Museum. Which, by the way, I think every lawmaker should have to do before voting on education bills. Dealing with a slew of other people's children is no joke!

The two times I was actually able to run to the bathroom I was startled to see that name tag staring back at me in the mirror. *Mrs. O'Keefe.* Honestly, it grew on me. By the end of the day, when I was dashing from the field trip to check-in on an event with which my company was involved, it felt almost like a badge of honor. When I finally made it home to my husband, he asked if I planned to keep it on when we went out to dinner.

With all the ups and downs of daily life, it's easy to forget that our relationship and marriage are at the center of it all. The whole reason our life works is because my husband and I can have so much fun and enjoy each other's company. Working through the good and the ugly is all part of how I continue to see how much I really like him. As a person, not just as my husband.

Just tonight, our littlest little girl's friend came over to ask to play. This kid didn't ask for our littlest little girl...*he asked for my husband*. And minutes later, this husband of mine raced outside to take care of that same little boy after he'd fallen off his skateboard and hurt himself.

My husband makes me laugh out loud, then surprises me with his compassion, and is so sarcastic I can barely stand it. Also, he makes me nuts because he puts dishes in the sink a mere three feet from the dishwasher (I mean really…what is that?!). But I adore him.

I love being a wife, and I'm so lucky to be *his* wife, and every once in a while, being Mrs. O'Keefe might be pretty cool. I may prefer Ms. to Mrs., and I may never change my name from Carrie Monroe O'Keefe to Carrie O'Keefe. But I love the fact that I am officially Mrs. O'Keefe.

What if throwing my last name to the wind sometimes is just fine thank you very much?

She Works Hard for the Money

Growing up, I tagged along with my mom when she worked on the weekend for her job as the Promotions Director for our local radio station. This work usually entailed concerts, giveaways, and parades. I loved doing my best to help her out whether I directed concert ticket winners to the VIP reception in the bowels of an arena or explained to people arriving at an event what would be taking place that day.

Because of these early experiences, I became totally at ease with event planning and execution. Comfortable with large groups of people and strangers. And a little more worldly than I would have been had she left me at home with a sitter.

While I remember those weekend adventures fondly, as a mother myself, I've kept our little girls away from my work. I've maintained that whenever possible, the little girls should stay home with my husband, or in rare cases a sitter, so they don't have to be dragged around with me for work. Whether for my actual jobs or for organizations I'm passionate about, I've been heavily involved in local charity events and not once have I brought along my little girls.

My husband and I want the girls to grow up understanding the importance of hard work and a strong work ethic. There are many evenings when he returns to the office after the little girls

are in bed, or when I'm tapping away at my laptop the minute
they are kissed goodnight. For some reason we've been
assuming that simply seeing us rush back to the office or work
from home would instill those values in them.

Idiots.

Fast forward to a weekend when we received a birthday party
invitation for my littlest little girl. It was on a Saturday when
my husband had school and I had an event I've worked on for
more than ten years. This left my oldest little girl with no plans,
and I had the great idea that she should come along with me to
help.

As the day grew near, my husband asked me several times if we
didn't just want to make plans for her so she wouldn't have to
tag along. I started to waver, but decided to ask her what she
thought. I told her that each year, I sat on the committee that
planned the Kids Race for the Cure. I show up early, help
prepare, work the race, clean-up, and head home. I told her she
could come with me to help or that we could find her something
to do. She nearly jumped out of her skin she was so excited to
come with me.

Saturday morning, she and I bundled up. Layers, and hats, and
gloves. Because really…why wouldn't it be sleeting and in the
40s on a mid-May morning?! As soon as my littlest little girl was
picked up, we were off. First on our list, breakfast and hot
drinks at Starbuck's. On the way, I explained that she was now
an official committee member and that she had very important
jobs to do. I went through each one and she listened intently,
taking stock of all her new responsibilities. My mom oversees

the committee, and my aunt is also involved, so I assured her she would know several people there.

We arrived at the Mall of America and found a mess. Winds the previous night had wreaked havoc on the tents and displays that had been pre-set. We scrambled to prepare for the families that would soon be arriving. My oldest little girl chalked the course while I helped repair the area. She's old enough now that I can give her instructions and she runs off to complete her tasks. She met up with the daughters of other committee members and continued to get ready for the day.

During brief moments for us to touch base, we hopped around and hugged to keep each other warm, before splitting up again to see to our respective jobs. When it was race time, I joined her at the finish line. She passed out medals to all the kids who completed the race, while I was the bouncer, not letting any children out of the closed off race area until there was a parent to match. As each heat finished, I kept an eye on my oldest little girl, and she was A- doing a GREAT job, and B - having a BLAST.

When I turned around after the last child had been picked-up by a parent, she was already hauling boxes and cleaning up with a new little friend she'd made. When I caught up to them, she exclaimed "I'm not even cold mommy!" I, on the other hand, was freezing! We quickly cleaned-up, grabbed our stuff, and headed for the car.

As we made our way to lunch, she started talking quickly. "That was SO FUN. I LOVED IT. We HAVE TO DO THIS AGAIN NEXT YEAR!" I told her she'd joined the committee and was now partially in-charge of the event and making it a success. That because of that, she HAD to help next year (schedule permitting). She beamed.

We had lunch and finally met-up with my husband and littlest little girl. For the rest of the day, she talked about all the things we'd done, how it had been so cold, but we toughed it out, and how my littlest little girl simply MUST help next year.

That night, after they were in bed, I started to think about why we've sheltered these little girls from our actual work. I followed my mom to work because it's what we had to do at the time. But the truth is, I really enjoyed it, and on Saturday I saw a glimpse of my oldest little girl feeling the same way.

She loved the responsibilities that were bestowed upon her. And I think she really enjoyed watching one of her parents work hard for something so cool and big. She hadn't been shy or unwilling to help at all. In fact, quite the opposite. She was enthusiastic and more than willing to do whatever was asked of her. It was cold and sleeting, and she was proud, confident, happy, and excited to be with me.

If we want our girls to grow up with a strong work ethic, if we want them to have a sense of our bigger community, and if we want to beef up their confidence in their abilities to do whatever comes their way, what could be better than putting them to work when things like this come up?! To give them some power in the real world and let them run with it?

What if I bringing the little girls along to work functions can be an adventure for them instead of something to protect them from?

Like the Movies

Phoenix in Summer. You know those rubber things you squeeze as a child and the eyeballs pop out? That, my friends, is how I feel in Phoenix during the summer. Dry heat or not…110 degrees is not okay.

I'm telling you about the weather in Phoenix because last Thursday and Friday I took a whirlwind trip there to attend my aunt's funeral. It's not fair on so many levels but I was very glad to be there, with my family, celebrating her life.

Unfortunately, on a quick trip to a restaurant in the mountains that is a staple of our family visits, I had an allergic reaction to something, and from that point forward I was stuffy, and my head ached. To sum up my trip, it was:

A – an exhausting 36-hour turnaround
B – hotter than hell (*not exaggerating*)
C – horrible to have my head stuffed up and pounding the whole time
D – very, very sad because we were there to mourn my aunt.

As my brother and I sat in Starbuck's, waiting for our flight, I thought a lot about my uncle and the challenges he would now be facing. *Without his life partner.* This sparked a recent memory of listening to the Katy Perry song "Not Like the Movies" in the car with my oldest little girl. The two of us were singing along at the top of our lungs, and on this car ride when I got to the chorus I got choked up. So much so that I had to stop singing for fear I may start crying.

Look, I don't cry. Like, at all. But damn it, there are songs (and one Budweiser commercial starring a horse…what?!) that get me sometimes. But this song never made me tear up. Until now.

There was a time when my husband and I had hit rock bottom. We were moving into a new house at the worst possible time in our relationship. I know, let's throw in a house move right when things are bad, GREAT IDEA!

The evening before the closing, while driving to the townhouse we were renting, I was thinking 'I can still get out of this. He can either move forward on his own or decide not to go, but *I* can still get out of this. This is a really bad idea. I. Should. Not. Be. Doing. This.'

I did it though. We moved in Memorial Day Weekend, and it was truly awful. Thinking about it makes me anxious even now. The weeks and months that followed were ugly, and so many things were wrong, neither of us was convinced we'd make it. I think both of us were fairly certain we wouldn't.

Around this whole move I'd find myself driving alone, listening to that same Katy Perry song, "Not Like the Movies," and start thinking about my own life. Because my life was NOT like the movies, but I genuinely believed that's how it SHOULD be. The song was hard for me to listen to because it made me seriously consider whether this relationship was right for me, for my husband, or for the little girls.

After the move, things with my husband got worse. We mutually agreed things needed to get better by a particular date. If they weren't significantly better by then, I was prepared to go.

Thankfully, that date came and went, and our life and marriage *were* in fact better. And they continued to improve over time. Thank you, therapy (and a lot of hard work).

When I was singing with my oldest little girl, I realized that the song used to represent a good argument for why our marriage *wouldn't* make it. But now, it describes exactly what we *do* have. Anything I thought we lacked back then; I now feel like we have in spades. Now that we're in a better place, I can remember the magic in the beginning, the magic of now, and it does feel like the movies.

In Starbuck's, about to leave Phoenix, I realized that you can't understand real loss until you have real love. My heart breaks for my uncle because I cannot, for the life of me, wrap my head around the idea of losing my husband.

Even now, there are days when I fear things will disintegrate. It happened once, who's to say it can't happen again? But I'm grateful to be walking through this life with this guy. I'm also so incredibly grateful that we had those rough times…because without them? I'm not so sure we'd know how lucky we are to be happy and at peace now.

Of course, there will always be things that fire us up. We will argue and butt heads. (Two Type A personalities under one roof anyone?) but at the end of the day, our relationship is amazing. And I've never felt so sure of that, or so thankful, all at once.

What if I take this time to step back and enjoy the good place my marriage is in?

What if, when remembering those terrible times, I focus on the good they brought our way?

And what if I do all I can to keep this relationship feeling "like the movies?" I'd love to look back at 50 years of that!

SUMMER

Hot Fun in the Summertime

By the time I picked up the little girls from the bus stop last Friday afternoon, I was exhausted. It had been an enormously trying week and a half at work, our basement had flooded, and we'd learned of an unfolding tragedy within our family. I needed this three-day weekend, or possibly a month, in Paris. But I'd settle for a week in Vegas or a day at the spa. Or even 30 minutes in a massage chair.

A couple of weeks ago, we pulled our summer clothes out and made an inventory of what the little girls would need this year. They are so tall and growing so quickly that it soon became clear that they would both be getting almost completely new summer wardrobes. We made plans that this weekend I would take each of them out, separately, for a summer shopping date.

Friday night, my oldest little girl and I went out for dinner and then went in search of the perfect summer clothes. She tried everything on, found the clothes she wanted, and we went home with two bulging bags of clothes and flip-flops to outfit her summer. My littlest little girl and my husband headed for the indoor pool and worked on underwater handstands.

Saturday morning, I took my littlest little girl to breakfast and then to the mall. She, too, found clothes she loved. While we shopped, my husband took my oldest little girl to the ceramics room at his school, and she helped him work on a sculpture. On Saturday afternoon, the little girls played while my husband and I worked on house projects. Saturday night, we all went for ice cream, read Nancy Drew, and got to bed early.

Yes, we did all that in one day, and woke up again the next morning to do it all again. On Sunday morning, the little girls and I were at Target a mere 15 minutes after they opened, eager to get grocery shopping out of the way. We raced home, put groceries away, and went straight to the outdoor pool. Which was followed by each little girl having playdates at friends' houses.

This morning when we brought them to their other parents, I was so sad to see them go. It was *the perfect* summer weekend. The little girls are finally getting less homework, the weather is warm, and we actually have time to allow them to just relax and be kids.

Today, as my husband and I relaxed for one last day of this much-needed three-day weekend, an idea started to form in my head. We live incredibly busy and fast-paced lives. No, not fast-paced like driving Lamborghinis, doing coke, and enjoying bottle service at clubs every night (did I just describe a scene from Miami Vice?). Fast-paced like trying to pack everything in that we can to get us where we want to be. That often means that between the little girls' activities and our commitments for our work and my husband's school and side businesses, we're running from sundown on Friday evening to sunrise on Monday morning without time to breathe. I don't want that for my little girls.

Don't get me wrong, I love that the little girls will grow up seeing their parents working to accomplish their goals and make their dreams come true. I'd also like them to experience what it's like to just be a kid.

I want them to know what it's like to relax. To know how it feels when the only weekend "plan" is to spend time at home. But if I want the girls to play outside with friends, end the summer with sun-kissed skin, sleep-in (even if that means 7:30am) and just *BE*, they should probably see their parents doing the same thing.

As I was drifting off for an afternoon nap (yes, I napped!!) I decided my goal this summer is to provide the little girls with a lazy, relaxed, carefree summer. One in which not much happens. Nothing of note other than just being kids. They deserve it. And so do my husband and me.

What if we attempt to have the laziest and most carefree summer on record?

What if our little girls get to have a normal, non-eventful, friend and water-filled summer? This summer is going to be epic!

Brave

Today was the kind of sweltering day that left us with two options. Either stay home with the air blasting or head to the pool. We chose the latter. The outdoor pool area is cut-throat. Mothers toting monogrammed towels and beach bags will straight-up check you like it's the Stanley Cup Finals if it means they'll get a chair. After four laps around, looking for any open chair available, we found one that was broken and seized it.

The little girls jumped into the pool, and we settled in on the side with our feet dangling in. They jumped in and climbed out and jumped in and climbed out, and on it went. We enjoyed the water and the sun for nearly two hours when the lifeguards cleared the pool. Several times a day, they conduct swimming tests for children, during which kids swim from the shallow end to the deep end. If they make it across without struggle, they receive bracelets that identify they're good enough swimmers to be in the deep end without a parent for the entire summer.

During the test, staff pull-out long jump ropes to entertain the kids who either aren't old enough or are not ready for the swimming test. Our little girls haven't felt like they were good enough swimmers to try, so today when the pool was cleared, we expected them to head over to jump rope. Instead, my littlest little girl called over her shoulder "I'm going to take the test" and made her way to the line for the swimming test.

Wait what? My husband and I exchanged glances. We've only been to the pool a few times this year and the little girls don't start this summer's swimming lessons until next week. We surely weren't expecting this. My husband called after her, "it's okay if you want to go jump rope!" "Nope," she hollered back as she kept walking. My husband followed and soon my oldest little girl did too.

My littlest little girl is the brave one. She rarely shies away from anything. My oldest little girl, on the other hand, gets a bit nervous. *She'd* already told us she didn't feel ready to take the test. But she followed my littlest little girl to the line and sat down at the edge of the pool. I watched it all from our broken lawn chair, protecting our turf, and soon enough my littlest little girl jumped in and started swimming. And she KEPT swimming.

She did the front crawl, face in the water between breaths, and it felt like I was watching an Olympic event. 'Can she make it?' I wondered. My husband, who was walking along the side, kept glancing up with a look of 'are you seeing this???' She made it all the way across and lo-and-behold, my oldest little girl was jumping in the pool. We watched in awe as she, too, made her way across.

Within minutes of when they'd walked away, both of my little girls had their deep-end bracelets, and my husband and I were proud, like they'd just won gold medals. What just happened?!

I'm not necessarily the kind of girl who plans and just does something brave. I'll ponder, talk about it, weigh the options, talk about it some more, and then maybe, just maybe, I'll do it. I can't think of many instances in my life in which I stood up, dusted myself off, and went off to do something as big as swimming across the pool was for my littlest little girl today. I need to do more of that.

This morning when I woke up, I hopped onto my phone, and checked all the things you can check these days. My daily games (I have to fend off future memory issues somehow), four email accounts, LinkedIn, and all the rest. The first thing I saw was a snarky comment about something I said on social media, posted by a nice guy I've known since high school. Which brings us to my own version of the deep-end swimming test.

When I read this online comment, my initial reaction was to think 'ooofff…what did I do wrong? How can I fix this? I bet *everyone* thinks this same *terrible thing about me!*' Over the next few minutes, other friends responded to his comment, and I convinced myself that I don't really care what he thinks. I mean, sure, it would be great if he hadn't left that crappy comment. But, I reasoned, I will not allow him to affect my day or my mood. And THAT felt completely liberating.

I went on to have one of those really great days with my little girls that I didn't want to end. The kind that makes me so proud and so happy that I get to be one of their moms. A day in which I want to squeeze their little bodies in hugs until they force me to let go. Tonight, I put them to bed, gave them their kisses, told them what I tell them each night, and came downstairs to write.

What is it about the evening and being alone that makes snarky comments feel so much more powerful and important than they actually are? I sat at my desk and looked around, avoiding eye contact with my computer, and thought about skipping a night of writing. Nobody will notice. Nobody will care.

But then I thought of my littlest little girl with her goggles firmly in place, adjusting her swimsuit bottom as she marched to the line, and standing and waiting proudly for the big scary swimming test. *She* didn't mull it over. *She* didn't weigh her options. *She just did it.*

And I followed suit.

What if sometimes I need to be brave and go for it (without over analyzing) even when it's a teensy bit scary? And just like that...I passed my version of a big scary swimming test.

Their Childhood

One summer night when the little girls and I got home, we called their friends to see who might be up for a playdate in the few hours of light and heat before bedtime. First call result? The friends were at Girl Scout Camp. Second call? Girl Scout Camp. Third call? Girl Scout Camp. Seriously? It turns out every little girl in our neighborhood, and quite possibly the city, is out enjoying the thrills of Girl Scout Camp. An experience I enjoyed myself when I was a little girl.

We gave up and filled our evening with other family fun, but when they went to bed, and ever since, I've been feeling a little blue about the experiences they miss out on simply because they have two families.

When four parents are involved, decisions aren't just made. They are proposed, debated, argued over, and finally decided upon. If no blood has been shed to decide something like, oh I don't know, what time works best on Saturdays for gymnastics, we consider it a success.

Since the little girls go back and forth between houses twice per week, and have to adjust to two different environments, and we all have to squeeze in everything a normal family would but in half the time, there are things we just have to let go. Take piano lessons, for example. Our littlest little girl has asked about learning to play the piano, but this might not work if she'd have half the time to practice each week. Because Girl Scouts fell on an inconvenient day, we didn't sign them up. So, they've missed out on the uniforms, sashes filled with hard-earned patches, the Bridge Ceremony, and selling those irresistible cookies. Knowing our unique limitations, we put them in a couple of activities per year and give-up on the rest.

But it still breaks my heart. I want them to experience every single thing they'd like to try. I want to be able to say, "we should do Girl Scouts next year so you can go to camp too!" I want our littlest little girl to try piano lessons, knowing it would likely help with her schoolwork as well. I want all these things and more for them.

But I don't get to make the final decision.

Instead, I have to figure out how I can be okay with our limited time and limited control over their activities and make our time together as good as possible. Maybe it means starting our own Girl Scout troop that meets on our days of the week, always, and works with our schedule. Or maybe it means more art projects, adventures to the museums, and concerts. Balanced out with downtime at home so they can run around the neighborhood with their friends. You know, when every single one of them isn't away at Girl Scout camp.

What if I try to recreate some things I enjoyed when I was a kid for my little girls?

What if I try to find the balance between making sure

they get to experience many things, and enjoying the downtime of staying home, in the confines of our limited time with them?

But here's a big one: what if I stop talking about how limited our time is with them and start talking about having all the time in the world? What if simply doing that makes it feel like we have more time?
Couldn't hurt!

It's Beginning to Feel a Lot Like Christmas

When I was little, right around July, I turned my attention to Christmas. Perhaps I've mentioned before how completely enamored and obsessed I can get with Christmas? I'm not saying I'm not a little crazy about Christmas *now*, but I was a lot crazy *then*.

I blame part of this on the boredom that accompanied my not being in school during the summer months. I was always thinking of things I could do to prepare for the holidays. One of my favorite activities, and my childhood friends can attest to this, was to play Christmas albums by the likes of Frank Sinatra, Bing Crosby, or Fred Waring and his singers, and record myself singing along. I was making these cassette tape masterpieces as Christmas gifts for my grandparents. I mean, what grandparent wouldn't want to hear their grandchild sing along with an album on a grainy sounding cassette tape?!

I started writing my Christmas present wish list in the summer because it would have been a shame to forget all the magnificent toys that are released in summer by waiting to start my list until fall. The real list-making-action got going after we received the five-inches-thick Sears catalogue in the Fall. But I always started a preliminary list in July, just to be safe.

I forced my friends to participate as I listened to carols, made gifts, and brainstormed my list. Which I am quite sure they *loved*.

When my mom met my stepdad, he made a ridiculous rule. No Christmas music or movies before Thanksgiving. I thought this was incredibly short sighted. And unfair. And cruel. How in the jingle bells would I make Christmas gifts and practice songs to get in the holiday mood???

Fortunately, he redeemed himself by becoming a real-life Clark Griswold. The man rented a cherry-picker to hang Christmas lights on the tip tops of our very, very tall pine trees. Each year, he outdid himself with Christmas light displays that would swiftly put any attempts by neighbors to shame.

I'm older now. My record player is somewhere in storage. I don't even *have* a tape recorder anymore. And I'm sane enough to realize that starting a list in July, one on paper anyway, would be weird. Even so, I am *totally there* in my mind. On Saturday, the sun hung just so, and it made me feel like it was one of those cold sunny winter days and I imagined my home smelling like cookies, cinnamon, and gingerbread. I imagined being surrounded by fluffy snow and I felt so joyful, as I do during the holidays, about being able to find the perfect gifts for those that I love and call my own. I wanted to listen to Christmas carols. I wanted to shop. And bake. And chop down a Christmas tree. Let's not forget the decorations, either.

Christmas is an enormous deal for me, but in the early days of our blended family, we haven't had the Christmas I expected to have with my very own family. Yet finally, we had a lovely, festive, wonderful Christmas. One complete with gift shopping outings that were so much fun, a fabulous visit with Santa, a great Christmas Eve with my husband's family, and a relaxing and amazing Christmas Day with mine. It was the first time in years that I felt like my real-life Christmas matched up to the

Christmas fantasies that swirl through my mind. *Six months out of the year.*

But some years are different. We won't have our little girls on Christmas Eve and Christmas Day this year. We'll have to figure out how to have a magical Christmas with them in the few days prior. It will take planning and compromise, and in case it you missed it, I'm not a huge fan of compromise. I really do like everything to be just so. And by "just so" I mean exactly the way *I* want it and the way *I* think it should be.

I'm well aware that I can sabotage our holidays by being sad about not having the little girls. It will be up to me to be sure we *make it* a magical holiday *regardless* of whether it happens "just so." As I walked through my office today, the sunlight coming in again reminded me of crisp December days. The Christmas mode that I'm in, however, will only last a little while longer. Then I'll happily return to summer. For now, though, I'm going to start brainstorming ways to make this our best Christmas yet. And I might sneak some carols while driving in my car alone. As I see it…there is never a bad time for Bing Crosby.

> **What if, since I won't be making any original recordings of Christmas songs with Bing, Frank, or Fred, I use my thoughts of Christmas to change what it will look like this year?**
>
> **What if simply having a different kind of Christmas can make it even more magical?**

Not Like the Last Time

As we sat on the tarmac waiting to take-off for Phoenix, I remembered another time I visited. It was nearly two years ago and everything single thing about my life was different.

I went with my mom and brother to visit my grandma and aunt and uncle. My grandma moved to Phoenix when I was about 8 or 9 and has lived in a retirement golf community ever since. She is a two-time widow and has lived alone in her home for years. 83 years old and she was still golfing nearly every day, driving, and living a full and active life.

This woman has an edge. She is not your typical warm and fuzzy grandma. Always quick to offer criticism when I would do things like…oh I don't know…wear my hair curly instead of straight on a particular day. She was never one to hold back her true feelings.

I remember telling my mom I'd be getting Botox the second I was able for the line between my eyebrows. My mom had been telling me it was completely undetectable, and that I was likely the only one who could see it. A few hours later, after she'd had a couple of glasses of wine, my grandma came very close to me and started tapping the supposed undetectable wrinkle between my brows and said "CARRIE!!! (tap, tap, tap, tap, tap) Stop scowling!!! (tap, tap, tap, tap, tap) Look what you're doing to yourself!!! (tap, tap, tap, tap, tap)" Obviously, this did nothing but strengthen my resolve to get Botox ASAP.

Later, on that trip, my brother and I were driving grandma's golf cart back to the house after going to the community gym. Earlier that day, my brother had questioned the fact that the battery on the golf cart was covered in green goo. Grandma assured us it was "just fine!!!"

About a mile and a half from home I said to my brother, "wouldn't it be so fitting if this cart died on us?!" Then three…two…*one*…and yep, the cart did, in fact, die. Some of her neighbors came to our rescue by crankily ordering us to get back in the cart and they'd push us home (because men over 80 are far stronger than us, apparently). The battery *had* died. Obviously. But my grandma was certain my brother and I had been tearing up and down the streets and that we'd broken it by driving recklessly. Because really, when given the chance to drive 12 miles per hour, who doesn't go a little crazy?

During that visit, she was more ornery than usual, more annoyed than usual, and more dismayed than usual. But this woman has always had spunk, and I kind of appreciate that about her. She was always so active, and doing her own thing, that you couldn't fault her for being a little bent out of shape when we descended upon her world, and she had to work around all of us.

Today we went straight to her new apartment from the airport. We weren't really sure if she'd even remember me. Since I was here last, they have moved her to a memory unit of an assisted living facility. My mom comes regularly, but this is the first time she's seen a grandchild in some time.

My uncle has been prepping her for our arrival, but we just didn't know what would happen. The good news? She remembered me just fine. She even called me "Care" which is what she's always called me. Unlike the last time, however, she's not living in her own house. Not golfing every day. And not able to be on her own. Yet she's cheerful. Disconcertingly so. Warm, and friendly, and cheerful.

It's not that I've never seen her like this. She always had her moments of warmth peppered in with her edginess. But it was never consistent like it was today. And while it's nice to sit with her and know that there won't be any overtly rude or crabby behavior? It also makes me incredibly sad.

That previous visit, I left my husband to go to Phoenix and our marriage was in serious trouble. We'd gotten to the point that I said by my next birthday, if things hadn't significantly improved, I would need to leave. I'm not the kind of girl to assign deadlines or ultimatums but if I'd learned anything so far, it was that I LOVED being a mom and I'm good at it. At 34, I knew if this marriage didn't work out, I would be on a tight timeline to mourn my marriage, start dating again, meet someone new, get married, and start having kids of my own. I realized things either needed to get much, much better or we'd have to cut our losses and move-on. For all our sakes.

Two years ago, when I was sitting on this same tarmac, my husband and I were fighting. When I landed in Phoenix and I turned my phone back on, several furious texts from my husband popped up. I remember feeling so tired of the turmoil and fighting, tired of trying to make it work. I was exhausted from the constant struggle, but I wasn't relieved to be away from him, either. Truthfully, I was scared that my absence would make him realize he felt a lot better when I wasn't around. I was suspended in the impossible contradiction of not wanting to be home, while being terrified of being anywhere else.

I spent my time in Phoenix inundating my husband with text messages in the beginning, eventually wanting zero communication about anything with him by the end of the trip.

Here we are, two years later, and I left my husband at home to work on a bathroom remodel. I honestly wish I could stay home to work on it alongside him. Our marriage is in great shape and I'm incredibly grateful that we stuck it out through really challenging times. I felt a brief pang of nervousness about leaving this time, likely leftover from those hard years and an irrational fear that when I leave, he'll think, 'hey this isn't bad at all!' And then I remember how amazing things are for us now and I let it pass. While he texted me pictures of his progress throughout the day, I got to revel in the fact that he's my husband and we're so lucky to have held onto each other.

Two years ago, my uncle had recently recovered from a severe heart attack. My aunt had been there to nurse him back to health, and he was finally doing much better. This visit, my aunt is gone. A horrible and unfair turn of events.

It's one of those times when adulthood smacks you in the forehead, or specifically on the wrinkle between the brows, and reminds you that you are not a youngster anymore. And it's both a comforting and good realization and a scary and disheartening realization. But it's the truth either way.

What if being an adult means coming to terms with how great things are and how tough things are?

What if despite the challenges, visits like this one are good for all involved, and I'll be so glad I came?

I'm Gonna Need Some of That

Tonight, my husband had school, so it was just the little girls and me. We rushed through dinner, reading, and math and then the neighbor girls came over to play Barbies. As I sat down at my kitchen table to get some work done, I started hearing rumblings of discontent from downstairs. Things like "we ALWAYS play at your house!" And "you guys are IGNORING me!" And "this is SO unfair!" Soon they moved outside where I could hear them going from yelling at each other to playing gymnastics, to yelling again, to showing off dance moves. Eventually, my little girls came in and asked if they could go to the other girls' house. I said yes, and they were off.

About an hour later, I heard little girls outside. I looked in the backyard and, of the five little girls that were originally playing, I now saw my oldest little girl and one of the neighbor girls sitting at our patio table having what appeared to be a serious conversation. Soon my oldest little girl came in and said,

"Mommy…do you sometimes need time all alone and by yourself?"

"Sometimes, yes. Why do you ask?"

"I'm gonna need some of that," she said, shaking her head.

I asked why and she said there had been fighting and she

needed to do some thinking about why the fighting started, her part in the fight, and if it was all worth it. I'm telling you; she is 8 going on 27. I told her it's really important to know when you need that alone time and to arrange for it. She said if she says she's going to be in her room, it really means she needs some alone time to collect her thoughts. *Her words.* Not mine.

As she headed for the shower, I smiled. Because that is *exactly what I need.*

When I was single, I lived alone. I would shop alone, get pedicures every two weeks, see movies, run, clean my condo, run errands, or spend an entire weekend binge watching TV. It was *lovely.*

I'm not, in any way, saying I'd prefer to be single. Being with my husband and little girls makes me feel complete. I love being a mom and a wife. But I miss the things I used to do, from time to time, and I hadn't thought about it in a while until my oldest little girl asked me if I ever needed time alone. Ummm…*yes, please.* Like, right this second.

It's been a long weekend and a rough weekend for my husband and me. We spent a lot of time in therapy back when we were trying to figure out if we could stay married. We haven't been in a year and a half. It's become clear, however, that we have trouble communicating effectively about certain issues. As I drove to work this morning, I left a voicemail for our therapist requesting an appointment. Which made me feel like a complete and utter failure.

Let me be clear. I believe in therapy. I believe in going back as needed to tune things up, make sure we're on track, and to keep communication open and effective. That said, I'm bummed out that we're in a position of needing to go back. Logically, I understand that will happen throughout the course of our marriage. I get it. But still.

We're so good about having honest and frank conversations about how we're feeling about things, how we're feeling about each other, and what we need to work on. We find ourselves a bit stuck right now in terms of understanding the other's point of view. Or, more accurately, what to do with that information. We're stuck on the "next steps" part. If you feel this way, I should do this. If I feel this way, you should do that. We need an objective and educated opinion. I know we'll be so happy to have help, but right now I'm feeling sorry for myself.

So that alone time? It couldn't come at a better time. After my little girl walked away, I started fantasizing about alone time and plotted out when, in the next few days, I can steal a moment or two. For a pedicure. A trip to the bookstore. To write. To work on some projects. This simple act of making plans for my alone time felt liberating and eased my stress a bit. Because we all need some alone time to collect our thoughts. Right?

> **What if, when life throws me a bunch of (stress-filled) fast balls, I plan some alone time to decompress?**

> **What if I remember things like therapy and alone time, while tough to get myself out the door for, will make life so much better?**

Mine for Now

Both my husband and I remember what summers were like when we were kids. The opportunity to spend time with friends, with later bedtimes, and no homework offered such unbridled freedom and joy. We remember what it's like to find great friends who live close, and we remember what it's like to spend months getting to know them and growing our friendships. We also really like the friends our little girls have made. They are well-behaved, and well-mannered, and have fantastic little personalities. We want our little girls to forge lifelong friendships with some of these girls.

As the little girls get older, they've started to want and ask for play dates in the summer. All. The. Time. Having the girls half of the time, means that having them in play dates for half of that time leaves us little opportunity to be with our little girls. If we had our little girls full-time, it would be different. They'd always come home to us. We would see them each day in some way, shape, or form.

My little girls are growing up at the speed of light, and it terrifies me. Each year goes a little faster, each phase passes a little more quickly. When they entered second and third grade, I keep questioning myself and thinking 'no…that can't be right…it must be first and second grade…right?!' Wrong.

Recently, I've felt a little sad that I came into the picture so late. I missed the first three and four years of the little girls' lives. Now that they're hurrying up and getting older, I've started to mourn the time I didn't get to have with them.

Last night my oldest little girl called me nearly in tears she was so happy. We all received the postcards announcing the girls' new teachers yesterday. Both girls got the teachers they had hoped for. We rarely talk with the girls when they are with their other parents. All of us respect that it's their time with their other family. But yesterday she called me three times with updates on which friends were in her class. I was so happy that she felt like it was important to share the info with me.

I know that once school starts, and the play dates become relegated to weekends, things will feel more like normal. We have a routine in place. We spend each weeknight together, plowing through homework. Our Tuesdays are crazy with the regular homework routine and gymnastics. We spend weekends running to the gym, doing homework, and all the other things families do. I know the minute school starts, it will feel like we have our little girls back.

This comes with the territory of parenting, right? Each year, your kids become less and less dependent on you. They do their own thing, grow-up, and eventually leave to begin their own lives. I get all of that. And I know it can be sad and challenging for parents to get their heads around. I get *that*. But I feel like they've only been mine for a short time because I came into this a little later in the game. I just got them. And what happens when they grow-up and lead their own lives and they have four parents and so many grandparents? What if they grow-up and no longer *feel* like mine? Or *want* to be mine? Because technically…they aren't.

I know, I know, it's a dangerous train of thought to entertain. Chances are, they will always love me as one of their moms. But this summer made me realize how much I adore being a mom. And a wife to a father. Them being gone so often has been a stark reminder that they will not be around forever. If I'm truly being honest, I kind of want to chain them to me and never let them leave my side, because then I get to keep them, and they can be mine forever. In some crazy fairytale world where I wouldn't get arrested for such things.

Ooofff…this parenting thing? It is no f*cking joke.

> **What if I do everything I can to enjoy the moments I have with my little girls?**
>
> **What if I stop worrying about the heartbreak of them leaving us (me) that is ten years down the road and just be the best mom I can be to these little girls?**

Bippity Boppity Boo

When I was a kid, I used to visit relatives in Cincinnati for a week or two in the summers. I loved visiting my aunt, uncle, and cousins, and my mom likely *loved* just a teensy break from my incessant talking. I talk a lot.

Anyway…one year when I returned home from my trip to Ohio, I found my bedroom completely transformed. New wallpaper, new bedding, and a brand-new look to my bedroom. As an only child, I spent a ton of time in my bedroom. Making believe. Talking to myself. Smooching my poster of Michael Jackson (that is…when not smooching the corner stop sign). Pretending to be a talk show host/news anchor/judge/lawyer/ soap star/etc. I read books in there, wrote stories, hosted sleepovers, played dress-up, and more. It was my very own little haven.

When I got home and my little haven had been transformed into an even *more beautiful* haven with decor that I loved, loved, loved. It was one of the best moments of my childhood. It was so completely unexpected. It was so beautiful, and it was *my* space. Everything about that moment made me feel so loved because my mom did it for me, and in a way, she knew I'd love. *It was magical.*

We moved into our house on a weekend we didn't have the

little girls. We painted their bedrooms light pink and light lavender and put-up wall decals of flowers and butterflies. One room is bigger than the other, which could accommodate a complete bedroom set passed down by my little brother. We filled the second, much smaller bedroom with brand new beautiful IKEA furniture. When the little girls got home, they were so excited about their new rooms.

That was three years ago.

This past spring, I started to get antsy about doing something to the little girls' bedrooms. Our littlest little girl has the smaller room. We've rearranged the furniture several times, but it still ends up feeling cramped. With not enough space, it quickly turns into a big, fat mess. She also is a bit of a hoarder in that she wants to keep everything. Packaging, broken jewelry, old lanyards that no longer hold whatever was originally attached. For the past year or more, her room has looked like a Bravo reality show waiting to happen.

Our oldest little girl plays school every chance she gets. Thus, her walls are covered with pages she's taped up (wince), pen marks from writing on taped up pages (double wince), and walls that have to be washed down regularly because she spends so much time standing by the wall as she addresses her class (of stuffed animals and dolls).

A couple of months ago, I started plotting. I'd say things in passing like "if you were going to change the color of your walls…what color would you choose?" I could see their eyes light up and their faces fill with hope as they excitedly exclaimed "HOT PINK" and "GREEN" simultaneously.

During a trip to Home Depot, the little girls and I detoured over to the paint department while my husband dealt with whatever we were actually shopping for, and we found the exact colors they'd choose if given the chance. On trips to Target, or while online, I'd happen upon bedding and ask the little girls what they liked and what they might hope to do next time we get new bedding. They'd scrutinize the shelves or the online pictures, ooohing and ahhhing while pointing at patterns they particularly loved. As the months have passed, they've asked when we might consider working on their bedrooms and we'd say, "I'm not sure" or "hopefully sometime soon" or "maybe when the bathroom is done." Their little faces would register guarded hope. They knew it was coming, but they had no idea when.

Because we share custody 50-50, we rarely have over four days without our little girls (thank goodness!). If we want to surprise them with anything big like this, it has to happen fast and furious. Because of vacations and schedules, we have a couple of stretches of time without the little girls that are longer than normal this summer. This, my friends, is one of those times.

We've had a week and a half with no little girls. Under normal circumstances, this would make me really sad, but this time we've been working on a secret mission: to transform the little girls' bedrooms.

Sidenote…all weekend I've been singing "Informer" by Snow but replacing the words with "transformer, you know transforming the girls' rooms while they're gone, a licky boom boom down." Paint fumes get to you after a while.

Ahem.

With the help of my mother-in-law, we painted the girls' rooms. Bright does not begin to describe these colors. They are so bright that at dusk the white ceilings take on a pink and green glow. My husband and his dad built a loft in our littlest little girl's room, giving her double the space. My mom and I tracked down the bedding they've been eyeing for months, as well as some additional furniture for the little room that previously was too small to hold any.

This weekend I made them custom switch plate covers (I am the opposite of crafty, so I use the word "custom" loosely), we adorned their walls with homemade art, changed out drawer pulls for new ones that match, and we've made the rooms look completely put together and totally specific to their individual personalities.

I'm so excited for them to come home tomorrow night and see their new rooms. Their own little havens. I'm so excited I don't even know what to do with myself. I was just telling my husband that, at the end of the day, I just hope they feel so loved all the time. And I hope this bedroom project makes them feel just that. So incredibly loved. If we can achieve that? It would be incredible.

What if projects that aren't huge in scope can do a bang-up job of showing the little girls how much we love them?

What if making a little magic for our little girls also makes our lives a bit more magical?

Old Enough to Know Better

Has anyone seen my husband? Handsome, 6'4", usually impeccably dressed, always with great shoes, hair a little unruly right now (he's getting it cut tomorrow), and likely rambling on and on about how amazing his wife is. Anyone? *Anyone???*

I emailed my husband this morning and told him it felt like we hadn't seen each other in years. Truthfully, I saw him just a few hours prior when he kissed the little girls and me on his way out the door. He's swamped at work, has had several evening meetings, he's in class three nights a week, is currently on call for Jury Duty, and for what seems like months, he's been constantly on the move.

He's been getting home with just enough time for us to watch TV together for a half hour before we both crash and burn. We communicate through email and text, reminding each other of things like forms we need to complete, things that have to be mailed, and calls we need to make.

Usually by the end of summer we've golfed several times, we've been to the outdoor pool at our gym several times, and we're at least two shades darker from all of our time outside. We've usually met other couples for dinner at lovely patios, grilled out nearly every night, and our house is in great shape thanks to productive weekend projects. Instead, we haven't seen many of our friends in ages, we haven't even refilled our propane tank this summer, and our house? I can't even get into our house (without feeling violent). It feels like we're limping forward as best we can, in a constant state of "We have to do this! We have to do that! We have to do these other things!"

If it were any other time and place in our lives, this schedule wouldn't work. My husband would have dropped the class (if not the program) by now, or I would have begged him to do so, and we'd go back to our regularly scheduled summer plans. But we're *so close* to the end of this chapter in his education. Soon enough, he'll be taking the GRE and making his way into his master's program. When I say "close," it's on the horizon, but he's still got a ways to go. But if there are opportunities for him to blow through some of his required classes (for example…two language courses in one summer), we agree he should pounce on them. The more we get done now, the easier it will be in the end when he's studying for that pesky GRE.

I'm gonna be honest. I'm not always so excited about this husband-in-school thing. When we met, he had no interest in a degree. Back then I was even up for a job at a local university, where he could have gone to school for half the tuition. We started talking about it then and the idea took hold.

When he finally decided he wanted to go to school, I was ecstatic. I went to college right out of high school, attended for four challenging years, got booted, but went back and worked my a*s off to finish. Ten years after I'd started. Finishing my degree was horrible, I hated it, but I'm so proud of myself for having done it. I knew full well this college thing might really suck for him, but I also know that my graduation day was one of my most cherished moments, and it will be for him too.

There are days, however, that I just want him to stay home. For his sanity, and also for my own. We already juggle a stupid number of commitments, on top of very full workloads, so adding anything on top of that is taxing, to say the least. Not to mention, these are in-person classes, not online, so he can't kiss the little girls goodnight and then head downstairs to log into class. His a*s is in a desk, on campus, a good 25 miles from home, several days per week.

But he's *doing it*. He never skips class, he has a ridiculously good GPA, and every time we meet with an academic advisor, and they tell us how much time he has left, he is positive and upbeat. Whereas I think to myself 'Jesus! Can't he test out of some of this bullsh*t?!' We now have a timeline, we know what's required for the admissions process for his master's program (piece of cake!), and by 41 he'll be exactly what he wants to be when he grows up. *Which is truly awe-inspiring.*

So, while both of us, right this very second, could probably stomp our feet and throw a tantrum about the amount of things on his plate right now, we really *are* old enough to know better. We know it will pay off in spades, we know the day he finishes his B.A. (and subsequently his master's) will be one of the happiest of our lives, we know we're on the right path for the life we want, and we have to be patient and accept the fact that some days will be harder than others.

If you see my lovely husband, tell him I say hello, and to keep on keeping on.

What if, even though going to college is an enormous time commitment, we do our best to enjoy this time by remembering it will help us get where we want to be?

I Never Want to Leave This Place

Two weeks ago, I was settling into my typical Sunday evening activities. Straightening the house, throwing in the last load of laundry, sitting down with a snack, turning on Real Housewives, and painting my nails. I was about to spend the week at home with the little girls, and thus, my typical need to get everything tidied up before the beginning of the week wasn't consuming me. I'd have *all week*, I reasoned, to do anything and everything my heart might desire. I had grand plans to clean this house as it's never been cleaned, to write every day, to organize my house and my office files, and to clean-up the online system I use for work. Plans to do all sorts of things that would make my life a piece of cake when I returned to work a week later.

Ahem.

I quickly learned that being a stay-at-home mom isn't all it's cracked up to be. The beginning of the week proved to be a challenge. Between driving here and driving there, dropping kids here, picking them up there, arranging play dates here, and sleepovers there, I could barely concentrate on any one thing before having to jump back into the car. How on earth does one keep their sanity, or get anything done, when they are the Julie McCoy, and the cab driver, and the personal assistant, to their children, 24/7?! As the week wore on, however, we got into a groove, and I found myself better able to manage it all.

Meal planning, mid-day trips to the empty grocery store, in-person registration for their activities instead of frantic phone calls, afternoon trips to the movies. I started to, dare I say, master the whole stay-at-home mom thing (as much as one can in just a few days, all while still answering frantic work emails and calls amongst it all). By Friday afternoon, when they went back to their other family. We'd done so many fun things. I was so sad to see them go. But because we'd been so active the entire week, my husband and I kept up the momentum, and we had a fabulous weekend.

There was Friday night, when I had the best golf game of my life (I'm assuming because for once I shared a cigar with my husband instead of just fanning away the smoke). And Saturday, we enjoyed a fabulous dinner and then went dancing until the wee hours of the morning with good friends (I never EVER do that anymore!). And on Sunday I went horseback riding with one of my girlfriends. It was the perfect end to a lovely week of vacation.

Then there was Monday. Back at work. And honestly, I didn't really know what to do with myself. Because I really just wanted to be the Julie McCoy, and the cab driver, and the personal assistant to my children, 24/7. Wait, what?! How is it even possible that one week, a mere five days, could have made me want *that*?! I spent the week catching up on my emails and everything I'd missed. We had a full weekend planned, and I was dreading it. I felt like I needed time to recuperate from my week back at work. Quality time to spend with the little girls. Another chance to slow down the pace a bit and just be around home.

I raced home through rush hour traffic on Friday, knowing I'd promised the little girls a spa night with pizza. I was wishing I hadn't done this to myself because I was tired, and it was getting late. I got home, threw the pizza in the oven, threw in a movie for the little girls to watch, and started sifting through the face mask recipes I'd found earlier in the day. I sent my husband to the grocery store for cucumbers (what's a spa night without cucumber slices on the eyes). All the while texting my girlfriend Holly about the 5k we'd planned to run the next morning with our little girls. Texts like "don't you hate it when you get home on Friday night and the plans you have just feel like a lot of work?" And "the run sounds rather early tomorrow, but I'm sure we'll have fun?" I think if either of us had said "let's bail" the other would have enthusiastically said "yes please!" But neither of us did.

The little girls and I first laid back with cucumbers on our eyes. Then we mixed up an oatmeal face mask (that, aside from photo ops, left a lot to be desired). I put them to bed with refreshed faces and plans to get up early for their very first 5k.

We'd intended to practice. I've taken the little girls on my training runs, but they always ride bikes while I run. We have a perfect circle in our neighborhood that, when run twice, is exactly a 5k. It would have been easy to practice, but we didn't. Bright and early on Saturday morning, we made our way to the 5k. The little girls had so many questions, and they were excited. The weather was perfect. This 5k was perfect. There would be "art stops" at which we could dip our hands and/or feet in paint and add our tag to large canvasses. It would be a laid back and fabulous introduction to 5ks for the little girls.

It was clear early-on that practice would have helped. We took many breaks to walk and took full advantage of the "art stops." It didn't take long before the little girls started complaining of being tired. As other runners lapped us, Holly and I decided it would be just fine to only do one of the two loops of the course. It was still an introduction to a 5k.

It still got them excited and made them feel proud (they even got race shirts!). And it still showed them, as Holly and I have been talking about for a couple of years now, how important it is to be involved in community events and to be active. The race organizers were kind enough to stretch out ribbon for us to run through as we completed our one and only lap. After all my b*tching and moaning, I was so glad we did it instead of sleeping in.

Our weekend continued with school clothes shopping (one of my favorite things ever) as a family. We always start with inventory, figuring out what we need and in what colors, determining what is passed down to my littlest little girl and then to the little girl of one of our family friends. Then we went to the little girls' favorite store where my husband and I pulled clothes like stylists. Both little girls left feeling so pleased with their new clothes and we felt so grateful that we're able to pull this off for them every fall and spring.

Last night we went to see a concert in the band shell at a lake. We got dressed up, headed to the city, and met up with friends. The kids played in the park until the music started. We ate too much ice cream, and we visited with each. We sat in perfect Minnesota weather, listening to music, and thoroughly enjoying ourselves.

This afternoon my husband and I were sitting in the house while the little girls and their friends sat in our backyard on a blanket under a tree writing songs. He was working on his laptop, and I was finally finishing a book I've been reading for a month. Classical music was playing softly, the breeze swept in one window and out another, and you know when you say something out loud without even having been thinking about it and you wonder where it came from? I said without thinking, "I never want to leave this place."

My husband looked at me quizzically. We'd soon be leaving for a friend's son's birthday party. That wasn't what I meant, though. In the past couple of weeks (since my vacation) we've done so many fabulous things as a family and as a couple. I often shy away from making too many plans because it feels like work, and I like the little girls to lie low. We've somehow found this balance between staying close to home and taking part in events and/or activities that are important to the kind of people we are and the kind of people we hope our little girls become. And frankly? It's been lovely. Although I sometimes get a little obsessed with things I want to change about myself, or things I wish I did better, or how I wish we could attack this or that project in our house, the fact of the matter is that I feel so lucky to be right here, right now, and I'm pretty pleased with the life that my husband and I have built for ourselves and our little girls. I never want to leave this place of happiness and peace.

What if it sometimes takes a vacation to remind me what it means to actively participate in life?

What if, once in a while, I take a peek around and revel in this fabulous life we're lucky to be living?

FALL

Talk to Me

I'll tell you what. This parenting thing? They should make you get a license for this sh*t. I am not kidding.

Let's pretend for a moment that you only did the bare minimum, and you focused on keeping your children bathed, fed, and in clothing. Even that takes thought. What will the temperature be today? Will they need jackets for the bus stop in the morning? Do they have gym or music today? Will they need tennies? Are there any special things happening today (i.e., going outside with the naturalist, Fun Run, science experiments) and what does that mean for their wardrobe (i.e., rain boots, tennies, hats and mittens, clothes that can get completely effed up without care)?

Now throw homework, spelling, and the obligatory 15 minutes of reading a day into the mix, not to mention the school paperwork. All the paperwork that needs to be sifted through, read, signed, returned, and so forth. (I'm absolutely sure my little girls' elementary school alone is to blame for the alarming deforestation going on these days.)

Not enough to think about? I have more. How about a few activities to make sure the kids can try sports, music, and dance? You've got hockey (what girl doesn't play hockey these days?), gymnastics (they *have* to try that!), dance (God help me),

golf (every girl should learn to golf), and swim lessons (so they
don't drown at the pool). Did I mention piano lessons, and Girl
Scouts, and all the other things that made *my* childhood so fun?

Beyond the activities, we also need to prioritize the life lessons
that shape and mold little girls into confident, bright, kind,
strong, independent, and amazing women. What about *THAT*?!
Do you see what I'm saying here? I once filled my mind with
the woes of the world, work, living the single life, drinking
cocktails, and shopping for shoes and cute outfits. And now that
same mind is suddenly filled with all the above. It's no wonder
some women turn a little crazy. It's hard to manage all of this
and feel sane.

For fun, though, let's add one more layer to complicate matters.
Try keeping all the above straight and moving in the right
direction, when you only have your children half the time.
HALF the time. I've said this before and I'll say it again,
sometimes it's enough to have me breathing in a paper bag.

Now onto the topic at hand…

One of my favorite things about children is their inability to
disguise how they feel about things. They are direct, honest, and
straight-up tell you what they want. There's no trying to
decipher what they're thinking. It's clear. I love that. I was
raised by a woman who is strong, confident, and articulates
what she wants, what she needs, her happiness or dismay, and
her opinions. I grew up valuing and, *thankfully,* having the
ability to verbalize how *I* feel.

When I got to high school and started meeting, befriending, or dating people who were passive-aggressive or just plain passive-passive, I realized I didn't really know what to do with them. I don't want to have to work to understand what you are, or are not, telling me. Just tell me. I don't want to have to guess what you want or don't want. And please don't talk in circles to get me to say what you don't want to. Ugh! I don't have the energy!

So, a couple of months ago when my littlest little girl stopped being the direct little girl that I knew her to be, and started saying things like "remember when we used to get ice cream? That was fun." You know, instead of just saying, "let's go get ice cream!" I was a little concerned.

Despite my having grown-up to be vocal and communicative, there was a time not so long ago when I simply wasn't speaking up. There were a couple of years in which, if betting on whether we'd stay married or get divorced, both my husband and I would have put our money on divorce. During that time, I became a relatively passive woman. I felt like any unnecessary rocking of the boat would land us in divorce court, so I chose my battles carefully, and most things hardly seemed worth discussing. Only the huge stuff felt worth the hassle. I sometimes wondered if I was saving my marriage or destroying myself.

I cringe when I think about how many nights we had this conversation:

Husband: What do you want to do tonight?
Me: What do *you* want to do tonight?
Husband. We're doing what you want tonight. Decide.

Me: I really don't care.

Husband: Decide.

Me: But what do *you* want to do?

A year and a half on the other side, I made it back to my vocal and direct self. But my littlest little girl seems to be taking on my old passive behavior. And it scares me.

When I noticed her doing it, we started talking about it a lot. My little girls and I have what feel like life altering conversations in the car. We talk about how we should treat people, what it means to be kind, and how to be strong and vocal about things that we do or do not like. I started talking with them about simply asking for what they want and need. And how it's so important to me that they feel comfortable enough to ask for, and talk about, *anything*.

This past week I've had a few interactions with grown women who simply can't ask for what they want. Passive, and passive-aggressive women who, it seems, don't have the strength or confidence or *something* to just spit out what they really want to say. And it is crazy making. CRAZY. MAKING. It made me even more aware of how important it is for my little girls to grow-up with confidence and the ability to verbalize and communicate what they're thinking, clearly and honestly.

Do you see what I'm saying? This parenting thing isn't for the faint at heart. It is ball-busting, back-breaking, mind-blowing, emotionally draining work. And if we're lucky, fingers and toes crossed and daily pleading with God, it will all work out the way we parents hope it will. Without us being put into straitjackets.

What if I continue to do everything in my power to help these little girls know their worth, speak their minds, and grow up to be confident and strong women who can verbalize what they are thinking without fear?

My Happy Places

When I was 18, I really felt like I was the sh*t. I'm going to be honest; my bangs were still a little fluffier than they should have been in 1994, and I hate to say it, but there may have still been shoulder pads somewhere in my wardrobe. But my Doc Martens and budding flannel shirt collection balanced them out. Every Sunday night my girlfriends and I headed downtown to First Avenue (the club in the movie Purple Rain, of course!) and danced our a*ses off. There was usually moshing involved (we were such grungy preppy suburban girls; it wasn't even funny). I may or may not have lost real pearl earrings in the mosh pit. We would walk in looking perfect (as perfect as 18-year-olds in 1994 could look) and left soaking with sweat, missing earrings, and with nothing but anticipation for the next Sunday. It was truly my happy place.

At First Ave. I was confident, and happy, and sassy, and funny, and could not care less what people thought of me. I was there to enjoy my friends, and music, and I felt at home. There were other places like that. We have a chain of lakes where I spent nearly every waking second of my summers. Rollerblading, cruising for guys with my girlfriends, and having ice cream at Sebastian Joe's. These places made me feel like ME.

When I met my husband, we realized we'd often been in the same places, many times at the lakes or First Ave., but had never met. We'd both seen the Beastie Boys several times, Stone Temple Pilots, Public Enemy, The Mighty Mighty Bosstones, Juliana Hatfield, and Prince. We'd even celebrated the Millennium with the same group of people at First Ave., but we weren't with one another.

Even after being together for five years, we hadn't been to any of my happy places together. When we go out downtown, which is rare, we go to nice restaurants for dinner and then to bars that cater to, ahem, *an older crowd*. Please hold while I weep.

A couple of months ago, my husband found out The Mighty Mighty Bosstones were coming to First Ave. Frankly, this happens a lot: we hear about an upcoming concert at a great venue and exclaim "we HAVE to go!!!" before quickly realizing we have the little girls that night, or we decide it's too expensive, or it feels like too much work. But The Mighty Mighty Bosstones are one of his faves. And as I've established, First Ave. is one of my faves. So, we bought tickets.

For our big night, we headed downtown to enjoy a concert we both saw in 1994 at the exact same place. Despite having grand plans to get gussied up in jeans and heels, I realized how miserable I'd be within an hour of arriving. So, I'm kicking it old school in Vans.

In preparation, all day, I've been listening to bands like Rage Against the Machine, Bjork, Beastie Boys, Alice in Chains, Nine Inch Nails, and Soundgarden. We're even grabbing cash so we can buy t-shirts. And I fully plan to pretend like I'm 18 again. I'm so excited about going to one of my happiest places with my husband. And I'm wondering why I don't make getting there more of a priority.

These are places in which I feel like I'm home and they make me feel like the best version of myself. Maybe I should try to, oh I don't know, spend a little time there every once in a while?

What if I attempt to get back to places that make me feel like my bitchin' 18-year-old self again?

What if instead of finding excuses not to get out and do things we know we'll enjoy, we just buy the tickets, and go?

Literally

I grew up twirling. An only child until I was 15, I had an active imagination, magic was a prevalent part of my existence, and I was a dreamer. It transformed every chore I did as a kid into a fairytale. Sweeping the front walkway? A concert in front of tens of thousands of fans…the broom serving as my microphone. Ironing? I was the maid serving a wealthy family and the wealthy daughter's boyfriend, also wealthy AND good looking, swept *me* off my feet and take me away. Setting the table? Preparing for an elaborate and fancy event. Vacuuming up and down stairs? Straight-up Cinderella. Shopping with my mom? Shopping with my two twin sisters, I would speak to them by way of the three-way mirrors in department stores, and we'd discuss the outfits on the surrounding racks.

I don't remember one time in my childhood when imagination and dreaming weren't a big part of it. When I got older, I stopped making believe (ahem…for the most part), but I never stopped dreaming. Whether it was of the college I hoped to attend (Notre Dame…and no I did not end up going…sigh), or the careers I hoped to have (lawyer/politician/talk show host…no/no/and no), or the kind of man I'd marry (George Clooney…and no I did not), or the kind of home I'd live in (anything out of a John Hughes movie…and no…my house is nothing like them), or the riches I'd earn and live on for life (still working on this one).

And while none of these particular dreams have materialized *yet*, I still fully expect many of them to come true. Okay, maybe not George Clooney. I *am* already married, after all.

I also always knew that no matter what, no matter the problem, the challenge, the obstacle, that I would always be *just fine*. Always. Money a little tight this month? It will come and it will be fine (always was). Car not working properly? It will be fine. Schedules not aligning? They will. I've always had faith that I would figure it out, things would work themselves out, and that in the end, it would be fine. *Great* even.

Let me tell you about my husband. He is grounded in realism. The here and now. The money we have *now*. The abilities we have to do things *now*. The things we need to address, do, accomplish, and attempt. *NOW*. I don't think it matters how long we've been together or what the future holds. We'll always be trying to figure out how to relate to each other.

The dreamer and the realist.

We look at money differently. We look at plans differently. We look at priorities differently. And, as you can imagine, this can be fodder for disagreements and misunderstandings. Yet I didn't fully realize just how much frustration and consternation our differences in outlook have caused my dear husband.

Not only am I a dreamer, but I'm also a communicator. This means that on a slow day, I could realistically send my husband 50 emails sharing with him the things that are fluttering about in my pretty little head. On a slow day, my imagination and dreams multiply exponentially. The more I talk, or email, the more big things come to mind. So, for example, maybe I'll start talking with him about signing our little girls up for the next session of gymnastics, and soon enough I'll be talking about getting them signed-up for ski lessons, and then skiing as a family regularly, and the next thing you know, we own a time share in Keystone and we're heading West each winter to show off our family's mad skills on the slopes, which obviously leads to spending time with the Kennedys…on a yacht…at Martha's Vineyard. To me? This progression in thought makes perfect sense. I mean, duh.

What was pointed out to me this past weekend is that this man that I love? He takes everything I say *literally*. I don't mean some of what I say, or even most of what I say, I mean ALL OF IT. Every. Single. Word. Which means he's wondering why the hell I think we can afford to get a time share in Keystone when we're paying taxes AND in the middle of a bathroom remodel AND taking on new costs with a new school year beginning, and so on and so forth. Thus, every email I send him in a matter of a day, all the dreams and ideas I'm sharing with him, they feel like reminders of what he can't provide.

Holy hell. What?! It has taken a full two days for this to actually sink in. I'm not saying I'm full of sh*t, or that I'm not serious about the things I say, but I don't mean right this second. I'm not saying I'm shopping real estate in Keystone right now (and who knows? We may eventually decide that Lake Tahoe makes more sense!). I'm not saying I'm booking a flight to Paris for this weekend. I'm not saying I'm writing a check for my Chanel bag even as I speak. I talk in *eventualities*. I talk because saying it out loud makes it so. I'm talkin' *SOMEDAY*.

I started thinking about how it would feel. If I had an overwhelming desire to provide for the people I love, and one of those people was constantly in my face saying "I want this, I want that, I want this, I want that" I would feel like a complete and utter failure. AND I would feel like that person will never be happy with the measly things that I CAN in fact provide. THAT is how I've been making my husband feel, not understanding that he *just didn't get it.*

Because *I just didn't get it.*

I won't stop dreaming. I won't stop talking about our future. But it's become clear that those conversations may need to happen with my girlfriends. Fellow dreamers. And perhaps I don't send him emails with every single thought. He doesn't necessarily need to know of my Macy's Thanksgiving Day Parade plans, or my idea about a jaunt to Boston, or the amazing Christian Louboutin shoes I just found. He doesn't really need to know about any of that until it's in the realm of possibility.

What if instead of inundating my husband with ideas of what I'd love to arrive in our future, I share with him how grateful I am for our present, and keep the dreams (or random thoughts about yachting with the Kennedys) to myself and my dreamer girlfriends?

Snap Out of It

I am admittedly unobservant. My husband can tell several stories about having done something in the yard or at home, and my complete and utter ignorance of anything being different. I'm also fairly unobservant when it comes to myself. When visiting a doctor about a sore shoulder or an illness, and they ask how long it's been going on, I cannot for the life of me remember. Recently, when my husband's cousin reminded me, I'd had lower back pain since we first met, I was shocked. I didn't realize it'd been so long. I simply don't keep track. I keep track of every other single thing in our lives, but for some reason, I can't do that with myself.

For all the therapy I've had, I feel pretty self-aware most of the time. I recognize my issues, understand how they originated, and know how to manage them. Every once in a while, however, someone will bring something to light that completely floors me. And I wonder how I could have missed something so big and so obvious. Today I had a conversation with someone that pretty much blew my f*cking mind.

In those early years of marriage, my husband and I were struggling. External factors we'd worked so hard in therapy to learn how to manage were threatening our relationship. I was also suffering from depression for the first time in my life. Each day, we grappled with whether we should move forward together or cut our losses and move on separately. During this time, we kept our heads down and slowly trudged ahead. Every day we woke up still together felt like a success.

When depression hit me, I was not prepared. I'm surrounded by family and girlfriends who have struggled with depression, but I'd never experienced it before myself. I remember being on the golf course one morning and realizing I felt completely detached when I was with my little girls. It was as if I was watching our interactions on TV. That's when I realized something was very wrong. I called my doctor from the golf course and soon began taking meds.

My husband, not sold on the idea that depression is chemical, was less than pleased by this diagnosis. I hadn't been feeling well for a while and, from his perspective, this was just another thing wrong with me. When things started falling apart for us, I started not feeling well. Almost all the time. Stomach aches, headaches, lower back issues, and I was always tired. It was also around this time I started struggling at work. I found myself less able to focus on anything outside of the challenges we were facing in our personal lives.

When we finally turned the corner after all the heartache, struggle, and hard work, we felt confident in the strength of our marriage. We were no longer waiting for the other shoe to drop, and we could talk about our future without thinking in the back of our minds that there was no future. We were *happy*. It felt, and still feels, truly remarkable.

However, my not feeling well didn't go away. There was always an injury of some sort, or something didn't feel well, and without my realizing it, the not feeling well just became a part of who I am. So did my feeling of being discouraged in my job and having the sense that I wasn't living up to my potential. My marriage felt back on track, but I'd been lost in the struggle, as though some of the really significant parts of me had been casualties to the rough years we'd had. *Our marriage* made it through, but the fabulous woman I know myself to be hadn't exactly made it through unscathed.

Today I had a brunch with a woman I haven't seen in at least ten years, which basically became a marathon storytelling to catch up on each other's lives. Upon hearing about my life in the past ten years, she made some startling observations that left me feeling incredibly unsettled, but also incredibly hopeful. Yet I also feel like a complete idiot for not having realized it myself.

She observed that when I met my husband he was at the tail-end of a relatively ugly divorce. Soon after, many more external issues became incredibly challenging, forcing us to focus on things that had nothing to do with our relationship or each other. Then, as we realized we were serious about our relationship, the focus turned to the little girls and how to proceed in a way that would be good and healthful for them after they'd already survived so much change. I then moved in with my husband and our little girls in what was once his home with his previous wife. I struggled mightily with how to fit into his world, and often felt like a replacement wife.

I've said before that in the beginning of our relationship, it felt like someone else's life. A life that I absolutely chose with my eyes and heart wide open, but someone else's nonetheless.

When we hit hard times, and we hunkered down for the ride, I started to feel sick and struggle with my job and suffer injuries. This woman observed that maybe, *just maybe*, these things that I alone was struggling with and that my husband had to pay attention to. Maybe they have been my way of getting my husband to pay attention to me. JUST. ME.

What. The. *F*ck*?!!!

She went on to suggest that maybe I was just trying to get any attention of my own, separate from our family or external factors, even if it was attention to things that were negative. Initially I thought it was crazy. Of course, I don't want that kind of attention. But as we continued to talk about it, I started to realize that this might in fact be true. Yikes.

She also suggested I may hold back to keep things calm. Something I know I did when we were making our way through the really hard times, but that I hadn't realized I might still be doing.

So basically, my subconscious mind has me A - trying to gain attention from my husband by feeling sick or hurt all the time, and B - holding back to keep things easy-safe-good.

I left brunch feeling horrified and sad, and I can honestly say that while I did none of this consciously, it absolutely hits home and makes perfect sense. When I met my husband, I was successful, and I lived life with joy and enthusiasm. I didn't complain about not feeling well or being tired. I didn't hold back to appease people or situations. I was ME and so proud of myself for being ME. And yet a few terrible years and experiences hit us and suddenly I feel like crap regularly, subconsciously use it to gain attention, and hold back to make things easier? Seriously? What?!

My husband was attracted to me for my ambition, drive, work ethic, and because I didn't hold back when going after the things about which I'm passionate. And yet, in some twisted way, I've turned myself into the opposite. I'm not saying I don't like myself, or that I lack amazing traits, or that I suck. I actually like myself a lot. But I *am* saying that there is some truth to my old friend's observations. And it's time to do something about it.

What if my suffering been a subconscious effort to gain the attention of my husband?

What if I need to stop holding back my full self to keep things in our relationship and family copacetic?

State of the Union

In most organizations for which I've worked, each year, the department or region or organization has gone on some sort of retreat to assess the state of the organization. Through reflection, team-building activities, strategic planning, brainstorming, looking at what we can do better, and recognizing what we do well, we leave after a couple of days feeling refreshed, refocused, and with a clear vision of where we're going.

I've been involved in retreats in the backyard of my boss' houses, at spas, and in Chicago hotels. Regardless of the location or of the level of swank, I always go into these retreats dreading every moment and wishing I could get out of it, and leave the retreats energized and ready to really hunker down and do great things.

Last week my husband and I tackled a conversation that has been bubbling. Not a bad one, just one that will take some time and soul-searching, and could be a big game changer. This conversation, because of all it entails, brought up many subsequent conversations about the current state of our marriage. Still today, a week later, new conversations are coming up several times throughout the day.

We've been through a lot, he and I, and we're grateful to have made it to a point where we're thrilled to still be together. We have so much fun, enjoy each other's company, respect each other enormously, and really, truly like each other. Like any couple, however, there are things about me that stress him out and there are things about him that stress me out. The good news is that we've kind of figured out how to navigate these things and really understand what the other is trying to communicate. Most of the time.

Over the past several days, we've had so many BIG conversations. Regarding our jobs, our money, our kids, our dog, our house, our future, our past, and where and who we want to be as individuals, as a couple, and as a family. I dreaded the conversation that started all of this, but now? I'm feeling refreshed and ready to get to the work of creating our future.

It's easy to lose sight of the point, right? With children, and work, and all the responsibilities that we pile on top of our heads, it's hard to remember exactly what we're running towards. While going through this process is sometimes challenging and painful, even heartbreaking at times. It's also incredibly necessary for us in order to maintain the relationship we've worked so hard to enjoy. And that? That feels like the most rewarding thing ever.

What if going through a strategic planning process for our marriage will ensure we stay on the same page and the right track to get us where we want to be?

Because I'm Magic Obviously

I don't FEEL magic. That's for damn sure.

When I was at Target last night at 8pm, struggling to recall why I bolted out of the house to get there in the first place, I felt like I'd been hit by a truck. There I was, in the same clothes I'd put on for work 15 hours ago, looking like I was half-dead. There were other moms half-asleep and shuffling through the aisles like me. Picking up dry erase markers because we'd accidentally bought *wet* erase markers. Buying new folders because, apparently, some of them only hold-up for a week. Desperate to find snacks that have *not* been processed in a facility that is within 100 miles of any type of nut.

I look like I've been on a four-day bender. The polish on my nails is chipped and dull, my eyes are puffy, and my hair is limp. I've fallen victim to yet another addiction. No, not Diet Coke…not even coffee…*pumpkin chai tea lattes* (there are no words). I find myself mindlessly driving towards Starbuck's in the morning, needing the warmth and the caffeine to even attempt my commute. And when the little girls are tucked into their beds at 8pm, I find myself longing to go to bed myself. Feeling regret for all the things that, once again, I haven't had the time to accomplish. And praying there is something, *anything*, on TV that is mindless enough to keep me content.

Thank you, Kardashians. Seriously.

And yet, each day the little girls head off to school with their folders full of completed and checked homework, notes to their teachers, and paperwork signed-off. They open their lunches to find healthful and yummy meals and a note from me professing my love, pride, and adoration. I whisk them off the bus and either bring them straight home to start homework or off to gymnastics. I have sleepovers coordinated a month from now, play date schedules plotted through November, basketball registration submitted, Thanksgiving plans in the works, and I was just thinking I need to start working on Christmas. Despite my complete and utter exhaustion, my looking terrible, my desperate need for pumpkin chai tea lattes, and my feeling so disorganized it makes my head spin (and hurt), I am firing on (almost) all cylinders. And from what I can tell, I might actually make magic after all (gasp!).

Tonight, we celebrated my husband's birthday. AND we had gymnastics. AND homework. And you know what? We did all that, and went out for ice cream, and the little girls were in bed early chewing vitamins as they nested in their beds. My point is this, maybe at least in this first month of school, my house doesn't need to look like a model home. Maybe I don't need to be crafty or organized like Martha Stewart. Maybe I don't need to look like a supermodel, cough, cough. Maybe my car doesn't need to be spotless. Maybe my bed doesn't need to be made. Maybe I don't need to go to the gym or run every single day.

What if maybe, just maybe, in the first month of school, all that really matters is that my little girls feel well taken care of? Safe. Secure. Happy. Loved. And while I would feel better if all the

above things were true, especially my looking like a
supermodel, ahem, all that really matters in September is that
the little girls feel like they're getting what they need from me.
And maybe that is magic in and of itself.

**What if what I'm doing is not only good enough, but
magical, as we get back in the swing of school?**

I'm Never Never Giving You Up

When I walked down the aisle to meet my soon-to-be husband at the altar, I walked to the song "Lullaby" by The Chicks. People listening to the lyrics likely thought they represented how I felt about my husband. They did, but we chose the song because the words perfectly described how I felt about *my little girls* – that I'd love them forever and never give them up.

I met my oldest little girl shortly after she'd turned four. I was hesitant to meet them. I wanted very much to meet them, but not until my husband and I were fairly certain we were serious about each other. I didn't want the little girls to fall in love with me, as little girls are prone to do with a new woman in their lives, and then walk away because the relationship with their dad wasn't working. My husband understood but, it also meant that I was absent from the biggest and most important part of his life. On the evenings he had the little girls, we either didn't get together or I'd stop by after the little girls were in bed. Mostly, however, we dated on the days and weekends he didn't have them.

It happened by accident. He was at the mall, asked me if I wanted to meet him there (knowing I would because I, uh, have a thing for shopping), and when I arrived, I found him in the food court with the little girls in their double stroller. My littlest little girl was smiley and eager to meet me. My oldest little girl was a little bit reserved.

She looked like a porcelain doll. A perfect little face, perfect plump little lips, big piercing blue eyes, and round rosy cheeks. She was quiet. She wasn't so sure. I kept talking to them (so nervous on the inside), hoping I could warm her up. When we parted ways, the littlest little girl asked for a kiss. I kissed her quick, feeling a bit uncomfortable. My husband asked our oldest little girl if she wanted a kiss too, and she said no. They walked one way, I walked the other, and I wondered how I would win her over. I heard some commotion, some wailing, and my husband called after me. My oldest little girl wanted a kiss, after all.

The following year was filled with heartbreak. She knew how to stab me in the heart just right. Whether it was crying for her other mom when I disciplined her, or saying she remembered when they all lived together and implying that it was better, or when we told the little girls I would be moving in, and she sobbed and sobbed and sobbed (despite their constant requests for me to sleepover).

Even though it broke my heart and killed me a little inside, I knew she was a child, and that it wasn't about *me*. I couldn't take it personally, even though it felt *so incredibly personal*. I continued to be there, I continued to discipline, and I didn't allow my resolve to be a good mother to waver. I was an instant and terrified mother, but a *good mother*, nonetheless.

She had always been a mama's girl. But it was her "real" mama that she clung to. A year or so after she first laid eyes on me, she became a mama's girl with me, too. The little girls stopped calling me Carrie and started calling me mommy (on their own – I never ever asked them to call me anything but Carrie). When we started having "dates" with our girls, offering them alone time with one of us, she started to choose *me* and not my husband. Every time. When walking together as a family, she would hold *my* hand. She began to show traits that *I'd* had when I was a little girl. She began to copy some of the things I said, some of the clothes I wore, and some of my personality traits. Things with her got *easy*.

Today is my oldest little girl's birthday, and she turns nine. We've reached a point in her life in which I've been one of her moms for more years than I haven't. She's turned into a bright, confident, kind, sassy (in a good way), and all around lovely little girl. And I think I can say with confidence that me? Her second mom? *I've* had something to do with that.

I look at her little face every day in the pictures that I have displayed on my desk and on my office walls, and I'm more and more in love with her. I see her actual face two to five days per week, and I can't kiss it enough or hug her little body enough. I'm so grateful that she considers me hers and that I can say she's *mine*. Our rocky beginning has turned into an amazing mother-daughter relationship that I wouldn't give up for the world. I'm so proud to be her mom and I'm so excited to see what this magnificent little girl of mine will become in the years to come.

What if a rocky beginning doesn't mean that's how things will end?

Storybook Sundays and Fairy Tales Forever

Last night, the little girls and I were on our way home from the gym. There is a home in our community that has their land filled to the brim with colorful sculptures. They line the winding driveway and surround the house. Some are crazy things we aren't sure of; others are things like peacocks made of branches and sticks.

As we drove by last night I said, "can you imagine how amazing it would be if you discovered a passion, like making sculptures and art, and could do that every single day?" The little girls were very excited by the idea. My oldest little girl, who'd had gymnastics earlier in the evening, said "I would be a gymnastics teacher and do gymnastics every day for like six hours!" I told them I would write stories and both of them were surprised and exclaimed *"REALLY*?!" I elaborated, telling them I would write stories, and write about our life adventures, and do it all the time if I could. My littlest little girl said, "that would be *so* cool!" My oldest little girl agreed. And I realized it was the first time I'd ever verbalized that dream in front of my little girls.

What the *what*?!

I've had a challenging few months. That's no secret. In that time, as we've struggled to keep moving forward with bright smiles on our faces and semi-positive attitudes, I've lost sight of some things. Things that would help in times of challenge. Things like DREAMING, and HOPE, and EXCITEMENT for the future.

Ummm, I *miss* those things. *A bunch.*

Today is the day to shut the door on the frustration, irritation, and fleeting moments of despair that have been hanging around for the past few months. It's time to reopen the door to imagination, dreaming, ridiculous bouts of laughter, and exciting thoughts of what's coming. For *all of us*. Even my literal-to-the-bone husband, who is *firmly* rooted in reality.

I heard a report a year ago about a newer school in inner-city Chicago that was sending its first class off to college in the fall. Every single student had been accepted and was going to college. Many of them were the first in their families to do so. When the reporter asked what was different about *this* school, and about *these* kids, the Dean explained that in many families in the area, college is not an expectation. Many times, college wasn't ever discussed, which subsequently meant it wasn't a part of the child's world view. If nobody is talking about college, or thinking about college, why would a child ever believe that it was in the cards for them? At this school, they made college a constant part of conversation. It was fascinating!

It stands to reason that if children don't hear or talk about traveling to far-away lands? If they don't make-believe or aren't encouraged to use their little imaginations? If they don't know that their parents are dreaming and plotting exciting adventures for their future? If they don't laugh their little tails off regularly?

If they don't see their parents treating each other with care, and kindness, and adoration? How will they ever know that such things are possible? Or better yet, how will they ever know that those things *SHOULD* happen?

Our little girls have four parents who are dedicated to furthering themselves academically. All of us have attended, or are making our way through, college. There are master's degrees completed and others being planned. We have conversations about how scary and exciting it will be to live in dorms. How exciting it will be to learn *so much*. College, for our little girls, is something that is good and exciting and important. I doubt we'll have to convince them of the value of education further down the road because it's already been firmly instilled in them.

But imagination, and dreaming, and joy, and travel, and philanthropy? These are things that sometimes fall by the wayside when regular life gets in the way. When we adults get bogged down with work, and relationships, and money, and responsibilities that sometimes feel oh-so-overwhelming. When there are crazy schedules in place, it's hard to carve out time for make-believe.

This morning I had an idea. What if every Sunday we have "Storybook Sundays" and the girls and I each go to our own little corner of the house, write a story, and come back together to read them to each other? Not long stories, just short ones. Wouldn't that foster an environment in which creativity is nurtured and celebrated? Wouldn't it also help them with their spelling, writing, and reading? Furthermore, wouldn't it allow me to write in a way that's different from what my other work?

I think what I'm saying is, wouldn't it be a win-win-win?

I want to provide a home in which the girls can dream big, use their imaginations, create art, and spin the globe and actually see themselves traveling the world. I want that to be their *normal*. So that as they grow and develop passions and choose their educations and careers and relationships…it will be built upon years of creating, hoping, and dreaming big. It's the only way their lives will have any resemblance to fairy tales.

I want to help make that happen and I could certainly use a refresher course myself!

What if we breathe some life, joy, hope, and dreams back into this house?

What if we set aside the challenges and enjoy our imaginations?

What if we can create the kind of world we want our kids to live in simply by allowing them to dream, make believe, and create? Wouldn't that be something???

Who You Callin' "We"

"Congratulations! You are officially registered for the 18th Annual Medtronic TC 10 Mile. We're looking forward to another spectacular race day."

Yahoo!

Sign-up for a ten-mile race…check!

Create b*tchin' running playlist…check!

Buy ridiculously expensive running shoes…check!

Start training program…check!

Take precautionary measures to prevent injury…check!

After weeks of training, forget to take precautionary measures after *one* long run, and get injured…*CHECK!*

When I woke up Monday morning, I knew something was wrong. I'd completed my long run of the week on Sunday, six miles, and the rest of that day flew by in a flash. I was distracted from my normal post-run routine of stretching and rolling the eff out of my legs, hips, and lower back with the dreaded foam roller. There was lunch to make for the little girls, and a party to get ready for, and books to read. I woke up Monday in a world of hurt with a familiar injury.

F*cking herniated disc.

Monday was a "rest day" in my training schedule, so I promised myself I'd go straight home to stretch and roll after work and then I expected it to be fine. I've run for weeks and weeks without my herniated disc acting up one bit. I was sure I just needed to spend a little time working it all out with the roller and by Tuesday I'd feel like a million bucks.

Only I didn't. I woke up yesterday, and it was worse. Much worse. I started panicking a little. Do I go back for another epidural steroid shot? I really *really* hated the last one (you feel cheated when you have an epidural without getting a baby out of the deal). It felt so wrong. But on the other hand (as my chiropractor Grandpa rolls in his grave) I cannot be going to the chiro three times per week right now for the amazing treatments that do in fact help (eventually). Not to mention, I'm six weeks out from a ten-mile race. A. Ten. Mile. Race. I don't have the luxury of time to just take a break! But oooowwwwwiiieeee!!! It hurts!!!

So, I emailed some friends…

WHAT DO I DO?!

ANOTHER STEROID SHOT?!

MAYBE I JUST CAN'T RUN? *EVER???*

When I'm whining, I rarely email my husband. There are a few reasons for this.

A - the man works his arse off from the time he walks into his office to the time he comes home. Lately that's been 7am and midnight, respectively. I'm pretty sure that if either of us has something valid to whine about…it's him.

B - he sometimes thinks I'm a baby. I think he thinks that I have no tolerance for pain and that I b*tch and moan about anything that is remotely close to hurting.

C - he was skeptical of this ten-mile, anyway.

D - we just made a $100 bet on Sunday that I would start lifting weights two days a week and he would start running two days a week, because we both do all of one and none of the other. We're supposed to start running together next week.

And finally, E - he's just not the kind of guy to swoop in and make it all better.

One reason my husband was attracted to me in the first place was that I wasn't the kind of girl who *needed* a guy to swoop in and make things better. I had my sh*t together, owned my home, had a great job, and was not interested in drama. I can hold my own and thus there are rarely times in which I need him to defend my honor or argue on my behalf. We're both strong, both opinionated, both independent, both successful, and both able to take care of ourselves. Which just makes us great partners.

If I'm worked up over something, he lets me work through it. He doesn't jump in and try to fix things (aside from my golf game…which makes me crazy). There have only been a couple of times in which he's gotten worked up on my behalf and they were for things about which he felt strongly.

I was reluctant to get him involved in the discussion about my injury rearing its ugly head. He doesn't believe in chiropractors (again, Grandpa rolling in his grave), so I knew he wouldn't be overly enthusiastic about a plan involving many trips to the chiro per week. I predicted he'd think it wasn't that serious. But he's been involved in my training, because it takes scheduling and logistical figuring. If I have to run four miles on a Tuesday, what does that mean for getting the littlest little girl to karate or making dinner or walking the dog? So, I knew I'd have to bring it up since I was scheduled to run four miles last night, two tonight, and four tomorrow, plus another 5k on Saturday.

I finally emailed him to tell him the problem.

Herniated disc hurts like a mofo, think I have to take a couple of days off, so discouraged about it, not so excited for another epidural, and maybe…just maybe…running (at least long distances) can't happen for me anymore.

And then I waited for his response…which I expected to be something like "I think if you run through the pain, you'll be fine."

Uh-huh.

Instead, do you know what my lovely husband did? He started asking questions. About the running, and diet, and the injury itself, and other forms of exercise that might be better for me, and about a plan. As you know, there's not much I love more than a plan. As I answered his questions, and we started talking through the options, I realized his responses were all about what "we" were going to do about this. WE are going to take a couple of days off, and WE are going to run the 5k on Saturday, and WE are going to see how that feels, and if WE find out that WE can't run, WE will go a different direction.

I breathed an enormous sigh of relief, and in that moment I realized I had been feeling like a complete failure, like I was giving up, all because an old injury was flaring up. Something over which I don't have complete control. All it took was my husband saying "okay…let's figure this out…what do *WE* need to do" to make me feel so much better about it.

What if I don't need to be needy, or a damsel in distress, to really benefit from the support from my husband?

What if facing this issue with my husband backing me up allows me to figure it out once and for all?

Past Heaven

The first time my littlest little girl told me she loved me was about a month after I'd met the little girls. We were in Target. She was still little enough to sit in the seat at the front of the cart, and she was parked firmly in the undies and socks aisle. I was a little further down the aisle looking for tights for the little girls' Christmas dresses. The ones my husband and I had bought together (our first joint purchase for the little girls). I was looking at sizes on tights and she screamed, "I LOVE YOOOUUUUUU." I froze.

Crouched down next to tights in black, white, cream, and pale pink. I wondered what to say back. I was very aware of the dangers of being involved with, not my husband, but with these little girls! I couldn't not say it back, right? But as I cautiously looked around Target (looking for what? People who would somehow know I was a recent addition to this family???) I was terrified that people would *know* I shouldn't be saying such things so early in the game. I said, in a little louder than a whisper, "I love you too!"

Oy.

Having just turned three when I met her, my littlest little girl was stubborn. She could stare me down, stomp her feet, and cross her arms with an indignant nod with the best of them.

Little did she know I could stare for minutes without blinking, stomp harder, and cross my own arms and nod my head indignantly. She pushed and pushed to see how far she could go with me and quickly realized it wasn't far.

She took to me pretty quickly. She snuggled, and kissed, and hugged, and kissed some more. With her I experienced so many firsts that most of my girlfriends had already endured with their children. On the way to daycare one morning, she threw up all over my (clean and beautiful) car. I didn't care about anything except for my poor little girl (this surprised even me). Or the first time I dropped her at daycare, and she clung to me sobbing…wanting me to take her with me. And the heart wrenching drive to work that followed. Because she was littler, and younger, and less communicative than my oldest little girl (who has such an old soul it makes her sometimes seem much older), she was the closest thing to a baby I'd ever had. There were pull-ups, and cuddling in bed with her until she fell asleep, and she *needed* me in a way that our oldest little girl didn't back then.

As she's grown older, her astounding personality has begun to take shape. She has the kindest and gentlest soul. She's laid back and is easy for people to get along with. She is quick to take people under her wing. She befriends those who need one. She sees sadness in people, children and adults alike, and immediately tries to comfort them. There are days when her kindness and love hit me like a brick.

In the past couple of years, we've had some challenges. Children are so different. The way my oldest and littlest little girls process information, react to disappointment, and do schoolwork is like night and day. Whereas our oldest little girl can zip through homework in the blink of an eye and catch on to every single thing with ease? Our littlest little girl has to work at it. It takes work to provide an environment in which she can truly focus and get through her homework. And there are days? Sweet Jesus, there are days that one sheet of math homework, or one particular spelling list? It's like pulling teeth with chop sticks covered in Vaseline. I've had to be hard on her, I've had to work to keep her focused, and it kills me a little each time because I'd much prefer to be snuggling or laughing with her.

I've also recently noticed that this lovely and kind girl is so intent on making others happy that she often forsakes what she wants to please others. This is a trait of my husband's. A trait that is at the same time endearing and the most frustrating thing ever. While it sometimes makes things *easier*, I so want her to grow up being able to clearly communicate what she wants, and what makes her happy.

Even though we struggle some days (at approximately 4:30, at our kitchen table, pencils in hand), she remains my little one. When I put her to bed each night and tell her she's a smart girl, a beautiful girl, an important girl, and a kind girl, and that I love her very much, she often repeats it to me as she strokes my hair. She often tells me I'm the best mom ever. She asks how my day at work was. She tells me she's happy that my job allows me to help people. And that I'm pretty.

The other day, she had her first day of basketball practice. A sport she herself chose to try. Without her big sister. On her own. Later, to celebrate, she and I went on a date to paint plates. While we were hard at work on our plates, I told her how proud

I was of her for being brave and trying something new by herself. How proud I am that she is such a bright and wonderful girl. When we were leaving, she told me she loved me, and I jokingly said, "I love you more," and she pulled out an oldie but goodie. Something she used to tell us when she was littler. She said, "I love you past heaven." And as we walked to the car, I struggled to keep breathing as my heart fully melted away for this little girl.

Today she turns eight (cue panic attack) and she couldn't be more excited. We often joke and tell her she cannot, under any circumstances, get one bit older or bigger. That we'd like to keep her at home forever. And she always joyfully agrees that she will, in fact, stay with us forever. And then she reminds us we have Sullivan, the dog.

What if I do my best to balance our sometimes-challenging times with the lovely times we're able to share?

What if I do everything I can to encourage this little girl to do the things that make her happy? And if I remodeled my basement to be a swank apartment, and locked her in there forever, would it really be considered imprisonment?

Vegas, Baby

Today is my husband's birthday. I can't tell you how irritating it is that he'll always be younger than I am (and that he reminds me of it often). Rude.

Monday night, the little girls and I were running our birthday errands. We tracked down the gifts we wanted to give him and ended up at Target sifting through greeting cards. I'm rather verbose, so the little girls each get him a card and I always get one from me too. As we were looking through them, and I was trying to avoid cards I've bought him before (or that were gag-worthy), my eyes fell upon a card with a Vegas sign, playing cards, poker chips, and more.

Vegas. Sigh. Vegas has long been our "happy place." Both my husband and I love to go. He plays poker, I shop, we sit by the pool, go to dinner and shows, and we're able to actually relax. We haven't been in a while, but it's the first place we think of when planning a quick vacation. It's quick, easy, cheap, and *hot.*

I remember the weekend I met my husband. Well, officially, at least. I'd met him previously, but I hadn't *really* met him. Our story began at the wedding of my friend April's sister, which I attended alone. I can't tell you how frustrated I was about that. I mean, I was so tired of going to weddings alone. Like the other weddings, I was dressed to the nines, groomsmen were hassling me, and there was nobody at the wedding I had any interest in getting to know better. My plan was to have cocktails, eat dinner, dance for just a bit, and then head home. My TV had a lot more to offer. (Or so I thought.)

As the cocktail hour came to a close, and the bridal party was taking their last pictures on the roof of the downtown skyscraper, other guests made their way down to the ballroom for dinner. Since the only people I knew well were the family, I headed to the bar, as any smart single girl without a date would do. I got off the elevator, and the only person in the ballroom's lobby was my future husband. Looking ridiculously dapper, hanging out and waiting for other guests to come down.

I said "hey!" feeling so relieved to see a familiar face, "I need a glass of wine!" He didn't remember who I was but seemed pleased to have company and I needed to waste time until the family came down to the reception. Or, more accurately, I needed safe harbor from the unruly groomsmen. And a safe harbor he provided.

This man wooed me all night. He bought me drinks, complimented my shoes, danced with me, came along to the bar after the reception, and when one of those unruly groomsmen asked incredulously "who is this guy…your *husband*?" he put his arm around me, laughed, and walked me past him to the bar for another drink.

The wedding was on a Saturday, our first date was the next Monday, and we haven't been apart since. And despite the heart-wrenching struggles in our early years of marriage, we stuck it through. Even in those hard times, Vegas always provided magic for us. At our very worst moments, when we were both sure we wouldn't make it, Vegas could still remind us of how much we truly liked each other.

When I saw the Vegas birthday card on the rack at Target, something came to me. The truth is, right *now* my "happy place" is anywhere my husband is. You could drop us anywhere and we'd be laughing, finding new places to hang out, making new friends, and finding ways to be successful in our work. Instead of writing a book's worth in his birthday card (like usual), I told him just that.

And I've gotta say…it's a lovely thing to realize that your happy place is exactly where you are, and exactly who you're with.

What if I celebrate my husband's birthday by telling him how happy I am that he's here?

Standing Appointments with Joy

You know how every once in a while, you have a moment in which you look around and really *see* things? Whether it's how much you love your family, or how remarkable your spouse is, or how much you adore your girlfriends, or how well you really do your job? I had one of those today. We went to an apple orchard with a pumpkin patch. It was 65 degrees and sunny, with a perfectly gentle breeze. I was standing on top of a hill that overlooked a park, hayrides, fields of pumpkins, orchards filled with apple trees, and about 20 feet in front of me sat a large group of my friends. Friends I've known since I was 12, 18, and in my 20s. And there we were, all looking down at our kids playing together in the park.

As I looked down, I thought 'this is so special.'

We've been going to this same pumpkin patch since 2001. When we first started this tradition, we would grab pumpkins and apple donuts, and then head back to April's house to carve pumpkins, watch scary movies, and drink. Now we bring our kids, and they get their little faces painted, play with one another, and we *all* eat apple donuts. Sometimes too many. Our kids know each other. Care for each other. Our kids know all of us and they know we are long-time friends.

On the Saturday after Thanksgiving each year, this same group of friends heads to a tree farm to cut down Christmas trees, buy ornaments, have apple cider, and, hmm, it occurs to me that we eat donuts there, too. We then return to our house, each car with a freshly cut tree tied to the top, to eat pizza while the kids run around our house like it's a playground.

I've said before (over and over and over) that we work hard to provide a stable and consistent environment for our little girls. As I enjoyed my friends and watched my girls carrying around my girlfriend's kids, or sword fighting with them, and as I watched my husband wrestling with my friends' kids, I realized how important it is for these things to continue to happen.

I want our girls to see good, strong, long-lasting friendships first-hand and to understand how important friendships are both for me and for my husband. I want them to be surrounded by adults that care about them and their parents. We want them to know and care about the children of our friends. We want them to feel surrounded by people who love them, care about their well-being, and see them regularly. And not just people who are relatives.

Having traditions like this offers *standing appointments with joy*. We always know where we will get pumpkins and that it will involve friends and apple donuts. The girls always know what we'll be doing that first Saturday after Thanksgiving (and that it will involve donuts). And I don't know, but especially for girls who split their time between two homes and two families, I feel like concrete traditions and the knowledge that they're loved by a small community is so incredibly important.

My husband commented on how great our day was and said we

need to keep doing things like this. Today I've been thinking of other traditions we could establish so they have even more things to look forward to and even more exposure to these amazing people and their amazing families. Easter egg hunts? Christmas cookie parties? Something philanthropic? I'm just so grateful I can participate in these things myself, let alone with my husband and little girls.

What if we continue to provide standing appointments with joy for our little girls?

Acknowledgments

I could not be more grateful for the people I'm lucky enough to surround myself with. Thank you to my husband Matt who sometimes believes in me more than I believe in myself. Thanks to my girls Signa and Sophia who are turning into the most wonderful young women – I love watching you grow and I LOVE being one of your moms. Thanks to my parents and brother for being constant supporters, cheerleaders, and some of my favorite people on the planet. Thank you to my girlfriends who offer supplemental therapy when needed, and are the funniest, tough-love-giving, compassionate, and fun group of women I have ever known.

Thank you to Leah Kent without whom this book would not be a thing. She told me I'd done the work (I had), she told me I could publish by November (I will), and she helped me bring this book into the world.

Thank you to the readers of *The Year of What If* and *Mamacadabra* who told me, time and time again, that I should put my stories into a book.

And thank you, friend, for taking the time to read this book.

About the Author

Carrie Monroe O'Keefe started blogging about her life by sharing stories of marriage, stepmotherhood, and how to navigate it all on mamacadabra.com in 2012. People said they loved reading the posts, so she kept writing. In addition to blogging, she released her middle-grade fiction book, *The Whole Truth*, in 2019.

Carrie lives outside of Minneapolis with her husband, two daughters, and dog Finlay.

mamacadabra.com
carriemonroeokeefe.substack.com